THE WI BOOK OF
SOUPS AND STARTERS

Over 100 recipes tried and tested
by the Women's Institute

MAGGIE BLACK

EBURY
PRESS

ACKNOWLEDGEMENTS

Illustrated by Vanessa Luff
Edited by Suzanne Luchford
Designed by Julia Golding
Cover photography by James Jackson

Published by Ebury Press
Division of The National Magazine Company Limited
Colquhoun House
27–37 Broadwick Street
London W1V 1FR

ISBN 0 85223 538 0

First published 1986

Filmset by D. P. Media Ltd, Hitchin, Hertfordshire

Reproduced, printed and bound in Great Britain by
Hazell, Watson & Viney Ltd,
Member of the BPCC Group, Aylesbury, Bucks

CONTENTS

INTRODUCTION

The essential feature of any starter, whether you serve a soup or a light savoury dish, is that it should stimulate people's appetites so that they eagerly anticipate the main course. Looks play a vital part in this. A well arranged first dish, garnished with care, promises delicious ones to follow.

Whatever your menu, the starter should lead into the main course. The ingredients should be different, possibly lighter, with a variation in colour and texture. A white soup followed by chicken in a cream sauce will make a drab meal, however good they are. Flavour and aroma are also very important. They should be interesting, but not too strong or distinctive. If the palate is stunned by hot curry, it will not be able to taste the later dishes fully, or appreciate them.

Another important point about all starters is that they should be easy to present and serve. The cook still has her mind on the main course, and may have to dress it at the last moment. Most of the oven and work-top space may be needed for assembling it. Many cooks today choose a first course such as soup, which keeps hot in one pan, or small cold dishes arranged on plates ahead of time to avoid last minute problems.

The plan of this book
This book is divided into two parts. The first part is about stock and soup-making, with recipes illustrating the main types of soups and their garnishes. The second part contains assorted types of cold starters, from mixed hors d'oeuvre and spiced fruits and salads to pâtés and mousses, followed by pastry and other starters served hot or cold.

Measurements
All recipes are given in metric and imperial quantities. When following the recipes, use either metric measurements or imperial: do not mix the two.

Eggs are size 2 or 3 unless stated otherwise.

All spoon measurements are level unless stated otherwise.

American equivalents

	Metric	Imperial	American
Margarine	225 g	8 oz	1 cup
Cheese (grated)	100 g	4 oz	1 cup
Flour	100 g	4 oz	1 cup
Currants	150 g	5 oz	1 cup
Rice (uncooked)	225 g	8 oz	1 cup

An American pint is 16 fl oz compared with the imperial pint of 20 fl oz. A standard American cup measure is considered to hold 8 fl oz.

SOUPS

STOCKS, CONSOMMES AND ASPIC

This chapter shows how to make a variety of
stocks which are the basis of all good soups,
plus delicate consommés (clear soups) and
aspic.

About soups

Soups vary from clear liquids to rich, stew-like mixtures and have many different uses. Concentrated stock sustains the explorer or gives a jogger a quick pick-me-up. A mild broth nourishes an invalid, while a hearty chowder makes a whole one-pot main course for vigorous youngsters. By contrast, a delicate consommé or velvety cream soup is the classic starter with which to begin a meal.

Stocks. Stock is a liquid made by simmering bones and meat, poultry, game or fish and/or vegetables with herbs and spices in water until their nutrients and flavour are extracted.

The majority of classic soups are based on stock. Most stocks need long, slow cooking so a wise cook makes large quantities at a time and freezes it. Stock can be reduced by boiling to a small quantity of concentrated nutrients and frozen in ice cube trays. It can then be brought back to the original strength and flavour by adding water.

Types of Soup. A broth is the simplest type of soup, consisting of the liquid in which the soup ingredients have been cooked. It usually includes solid pieces of the ingredients themselves, as well as added ones.

A clear soup or consommé is a strong, clarified stock, flavoured and garnished to stimulate the appetite. It is therefore most often used as a starter. In hot weather, it may be served chilled and jellied.

A puréed soup is thickened to a creamy consistency by reducing the main soup ingredients to a pulp and returning them to the cooking liquid.

A thickened soup is made with a thickening agent, usually a cereal, as well as, or instead of, a purée.

A cream soup is made by adding cream, and sometimes beaten egg yolk, to any puréed or thickened soup. A shellfish-based cream soup is called a bisque.

Ingredients. Besides a stock or other liquid base flavouring ingredients are generally needed for the particular soup being made. The concentrated liquid from cooking can be used, but more often sliced, chopped or puréed solid ingredients are added, reserving a few choice pieces for garnishing.

A puréed soup made with potatoes or pulses does not, as a rule, need extra thickening. The most usual thickening agent added to other soups is a powdered or mealy grain such as plain flour, cornflour or ground rice, or a puréed, softened grain, potato or pulse. Other thickening agents more rarely used are soft breadcrumbs or (for hare soup) blood. Beaten egg and milk or cream may be used which gives a rich and velvety consistency, or in a few special soups, yoghurt.

Flour or a similar thickening agent may be added to a soup in various ways. It can be creamed with a little cold liquid, stirred into the hot soup, and brought to the boil for a few moments. Alternatively, it can be blended with fat as beurre manié, stirred into the soup just below boiling point and allowed to dissolve before boiling. It can be cooked with fat as in a white or brown roux and blended with a little hot soup before stirring into the main soup. Pulses or breadcrumbs are generally added to the soup on their own, and are cooked with it for a while to blend in. Cream, egg, yoghurt or blood are added to the completed soup, off the boil; it must not be boiled again or they will curdle.

Extra ingredients are sometimes added to a soup, to give it body or flavour, or to garnish it and improve the appearance. For instance, pasta is added to minestrone, port or sherry may be added to a game soup, or diced cooked vegetables to a consommé.

Garnishes. These give soups personality, providing contrasting textures, shapes, and often flavours.

They may be added to the soup just before serving or be served with it for people to add themselves. Certain accompaniments are also commonly served with soups. Some classic garnishes and accompaniments are described on pages 33–36 below.

Equipment. A large stew-pan or preserving pan which can be tightly covered is a must for making a practical quantity of meat stock to store, although a small quantity can be made in a large pan. The only special equipment essential for classic soup-making is a jelly bag or muslin-lined round-bottomed strainer for clarifying stock for consommés. A food processor or blender, or a food mill which shreds, grates or sieves raw or cooked vegetables saves a great deal of time and work. If sieving is done by hand, a modern stainless metal or hard-meshed nylon sieve makes the task quicker and easier. The cooking time is also much shorter if soups are made in a pressure cooker or a microwave oven.

Quantities to serve. This will depend both on the type of soup and on the occasion. Only 150 ml (¼ pint) of a delicate consommée may be needed if used as a starter before a long or formal menu, while 275 ml (½ pint) or more may be needed of a hearty main-course broth or chowder (fish and potato soup). About 200 ml (⅓ pint) makes an average serving of most other soups.

Serving. Most hot soups are best served heated in deep plates or wide bowls, but consommés and all cold and jellied soups should be offered in small bowls or soup cups. Cold soups can be ladled into chilled cups ahead of time and refrigerated, but a hot soup is best brought to the table in a tureen or casserole. If there is any uncertainty about the starting time of the meal, it can be kept hot in a large vacuum flask.

CHICKEN STOCK

Makes 2 litres (3½ pints)

2 dried bay leaves
3 sprigs parsley
6 white peppercorns
4 litres (7 pints) water
½ large boiling chicken, skinned and
* jointed (1.1 kg/2½ lb)*
chicken giblets (minus liver and
* kidneys)*
4 medium carrots (optional)
4 celery stalks with leaves, cut in
* short lengths*
4 medium onions, peeled and
* quartered*
salt

Loosely tie the herbs in muslin. Place all the ingredients in a large pan. Bring to the boil and skim off any fat or scum. Reduce the heat, cover, and simmer for about 3 hours. Stir occasionally, and skim frequently.

Cool slightly, then strain into a clean bowl. Stand the bowl in chilled water until the stock is cold. Refrigerate, covered, until any fat on the surface is hard. Remove the fat and chill or freeze the stock until required.

Chicken stock can also be made with the carcase of a whole roasted bird and any scraps and skin. Use only 1.2 litres (2 pints) water and half the flavouring vegetables, herbs and spices.

Variation
Classic (but expensive) white stock is made with 900 g (2 lb) veal bones or knuckle, 2.3 litres (4 pints) water, and half the flavouring vegetables, herbs and spices above. Add 1–2 tsp lemon juice and simmer as above for at least 4 hours. This stock makes a good base for aspic jelly.

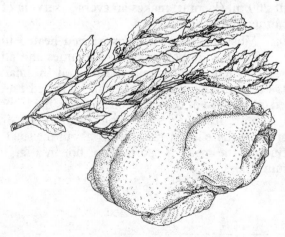

BASIC BROWN STOCK

Makes 2.8 litres (5 pints)

*350 g (¾ lb) chicken carcase or
  bones*
*900 g (2 lb) beef bones, sawn into
  short pieces*
*700 g (1 ½ lb) stewing beef (flank or
  skirt) cut into small pieces*
350 g (12 oz) onions, quartered
2 medium carrots, thickly sliced
*1 outside celery stalk, cut into 2 cm
  (¾ in) lengths*
5 sprigs parsley
2 fresh or 1 dried bay leaf
*2 sprigs fresh thyme or rosemary if
  available*
4 litres (7 pints) water
salt

Heat the oven 220°C (425°F) mark 7.
Spread out the carcase, bones and meat in
a large roasting tin, and roast for 30–40
minutes. Halfway through, turn the bones
and meat over. Prepare the vegetables and
add the onions and carrots to the pan with
the herb loosely tied in muslin.

Transfer the bones and meat to a large
pan. Add 275 ml (½ pint) water to the tin,
and place over a moderate heat. Stir with a
metal spoon to loosen any sediment. Pour
the liquids into the pan, add the rest of the
water and the other ingredients. Bring to
the boil, skim well, then reduce the heat,
cover and simmer for 4 hours. Remove the
bones and strain the stock through a fine
sieve into a heat-proof bowl. Re-season if
necessary. Stand the bowl in chilled water.
Refrigerate when cool enough. Remove any
fat from the surface when hardened, and
chill or freeze the stock until wanted.

Variation
For quick household stock, for everyday
use, collect the bones from any brown
poultry or any game bird or animal, as well
as trimmings from a chicken carcase and
add to the beef bones. Freeze in a plastic
bag until needed, then add root vegetables,
herbs and flavourings (not green vegetables,
potatoes or pulses). Use the same
proportions of solids and water as for basic
brown stock (above). Simmer (without
browning first) then strain, cool and store as
for basic brown stock. Household stock is
useful for family soups and stews, but for
starter and more luxurious soups, use basic
brown stock.

For jellied stock or consommé include
some veal bones when making brown stock.

FISH STOCK

Makes 1.5 litres (2½ pints)

900 g (2 lb) heads, bones and
*   trimmings of white fish*
juice of 1 large lemon
2 large onions, peeled and quartered
3 celery stalks, cut in 5 cm (2 in)
*   lengths*
1 medium sized carrot, quartered
1 fresh or ½ dried bay leaf
10 white peppercorns
6 parsley stalks
1 sprig fresh thyme if available
1.5 litres (2½ pints) water
salt

Place all the ingredients in a large pan, using enough water to cover the solids. Bring to the boil, then reduce the heat and simmer gently, uncovered, for 30 minutes. Skim as needed while cooking.

Soak a double layer of muslin in cold water and wring it out. Use to line a colander placed over a heat-proof bowl. Strain the stock through the muslin into the bowl. Stand the bowl in chilled water and stir until the stock is tepid. Season lightly. Leave until cold, then cover and refrigerate or freeze.

BASIC VEGETABLE STOCK

Makes 1.75 litres (3 pints)

5 small onions, peeled and halved
5 medium carrots, halved
4 medium tomatoes, quartered
½ clove garlic, squeezed over the
*   tomatoes*
3 small celery stalks, cut in 2 cm
*   (¾ in) lengths*
6–8 parsley stalks
2 litres (3½ pints) water

Place all the ingredients in a large pan, making sure that the water covers the solids. Bring to the boil. Reduce the heat, cover, and simmer for 1 hour.

Leave to stand off the heat for 30 minutes. Strain through a colander lined with damp muslin into a suitable container. Cool by standing the container in chilled water until cold. Use the same day if not refrigerated. Chill, covered, for 2 days only, or freeze for up to 2 months.

BROWN VEGETABLE STOCK

Makes 2 litres (3½ pints)

25 g (1 oz) margarine
3 small onions, quartered
3 medium-sized carrots, sliced
2 outside stalks celery, sliced
2 tomatoes, sliced
6 parsley stalks
1 fresh or ½ dried bay leaf
6 black peppercorns
1 whole blade mace
lemon juice to taste
2 litres (3½ pints) boiling water
salt

Heat the margarine in a pan. Add the onions, carrots and celery, and stir-fry until the vegetables are lightly browned. Add all the remaining ingredients except the salt. Bring to the boil. Reduce the heat, cover and simmer for 1 hour. Leave to stand off the heat for 20 minutes. Strain through a colander lined with damp muslin into a bowl. Season. Cool completely, then remove any fat from the surface. Chill for 2 days or freeze for up to 2 months.

CLASSIC CONSOMME

Makes 1 litre (1¾ pints)

1.2 litres (2 pints) basic brown stock (see page 11)
100 g (4 oz) shin of beef
150 ml (¼ pint) cold water
1 small onion, peeled and quartered
1 small carrot, scraped and quartered
1 small stalk of celery, sliced
bouquet garni
¼ tsp salt
2–3 white peppercorns
white and crushed shell of 1 egg
2 tsp dry sherry or Madeira (optional)

Ensure that the pan, jelly bag or wire sieve lined with muslin, and any spoon or bowls are quite free from grease. Strain the brown stock into the clean pan to remove any fat droplets. Shred the meat, removing any fat, and soak in the water for 15 minutes. Prepare the vegetables while the meat is soaking. Place the meat, water, vegetables, bouquet garni and seasonings into the pan with the stock. Add the egg white and shell to clear the stock. Heat gently, whisking continuously, until a thick froth forms on the surface. Remove the whisk and bring to simmering point; reduce the heat at once, cover the pan, and simmer very gently for 1½–2 hours. Do not boil or the froth will break up and cloud the consommé.

Scald a jelly bag or clean cloth. Tie it to the legs of an upturned stool to hold open. Filter the stock through gently, into a clean bowl, holding back the froth with a spoon at first, then letting it slide through on to the cloth. Pour the stock through the bag and egg white filter a second time into a second (white) bowl. The stock should be sparklingly clear; this is easy to see in the white bowl. Reheat, and season or flavour with alcohol if you wish; or cool, covered, then chill if wanted cold.

Variations
To make jellied consommé use brown stock (see page 11) made with veal bones. A cheaper, simpler alternative is to stir a little dissolved gelatine into the consommé before cooling; however the soup is then less clear and becomes cloudy when frozen.

Consommés often take their name from their garnishes. To prevent the garnish from clouding the consommé, rinse it before adding to the soup.
　　Here are some classic garnishes for 1 litre (1¾ pints) of consommé.
Consommé jardinière. Prepare about 6 tbsp of jardinière vegetables (carrot, turnip, cauliflower, small green peas or beans). Cut the carrot and the turnip into pea-sized ball shapes, with a very small vegetable baller, or cut into very small dice. Cut the cauliflower into tiny sprigs. Choose small peas or cut young, thin green beans into diamond shapes by slicing diagonally. Cook the vegetables for a few minutes in unsalted boiling water, drain and season lightly. To serve, place in a warmed tureen or into soup bowls or cups. Pour the hot consommé over the vegetables.
Consommé julienne. Prepare about 6 tbsp julienne vegetables. Using the largest holes on a grater, cut vegetables such as carrot

and turnip into coarse shreds 2–3 cm
(¾–1½ in) long. Finely slice the white of
leek or celery. Boil the vegetables separately
until just tender, season lightly, rinse and
serve as for jardinière vegetables (see
opposite).

Julienne means thin matchstick shapes or
very fine shreds of vegetables. Use as a
garnish in many dishes or serve as a cold
hors d'oeuvre or as a hot vegetable.

Consommé brunoise. Prepare a mixture of
4–6 tbsp diced carrot and turnip and sliced
leek and celery. Boil, season and rinse,
serve as for jardinière vegetables (see
opposite).

Consommé mimosa. Press 3–4 hard-boiled
egg yolks through a coarse sieve into the
consommé (almost at boiling point) just
before serving.

Consommé royale. Make a steamed savoury
egg custard as follows. Beat 1 egg yolk with
1 tbsp stock, milk or cream until fully
blended. Season lightly. Strain into a small,
greased heat-proof container, cover tightly
with foil or greaseproof paper, and steam
the custard until firm in a pan of gently
simmering water. Cool the custard, turn it
out, cut into thin slices, and then into
rounds, lozenge or other fancy shapes. Add
to the consommé just before serving.

Royale custard can be coloured with beet
juice, tomato juice etc. Coloured royale
shapes are part of the garnish of a number of
consommés.

Consommé printanier. Prepare a mixture of
about 6 tbsp small carrot and turnip balls as
for jardinière vegetables (see opposite),
small young cooked green peas and finely
shredded lettuce. Serve as for consommé
jardinière.

Consommé Solange. Add 2 tbsp rinsed, cooked pearl barley and 2 tbsp julienne of cooked chicken with a few small squares of rinsed lettuce to the consommé just before serving.

Clear mock turtle soup. Clear mock turtle soup consists of white stock (made with veal bones or knuckle, see page 10) cleared in the same way as consommé.

Add 50 ml (2 fl oz) sherry and 2 tsp lemon juice to each litre (1¾ pints) of cleared soup before reheating. After reheating add diced cooked veal as a garnish.

ASPIC JELLY

Makes 1 litre (1¾ pints) jelly

2 dried bay leaves
sprig of thyme
1 strip lemon rind
6 black peppercorns
1 litre (1¾ pints) cold white or basic brown stock (see pages 10 and 11)
120 ml (4 fl oz) white wine or half white wine and half dry sherry (with brown stock)
2 tbsp white wine vinegar
40 g (1½ oz gelatine)
whites and crushed shells of 2 eggs

Tie the bay leaves, thyme, lemon rind and peppercorns loosely in a muslin bag. Skim any fat from the stock. Place in a large scalded pan (not aluminium) with all the other ingredients. Stir with a scalded whisk until the gelatine softens. Heat, whisking constantly until simmering point is reached. Remove the whisk. When the liquid boils up, remove the pan from the heat. Allow to stand for a few moments, taking care not to break the crust formed by the egg white. The egg white traps the sediment in the stock and clears the aspic. Strain gently through a jelly bag as for consommé (see page 13), without breaking the egg white crust. If required strain through the crust a second time. The jelly must be quite clear. Cool, then chill. Test for firmness.

MEAT, POULTRY AND FISH SOUPS

This chapter contains an interesting and varied
selection of recipes which make the most of
meat, fish and poultry.

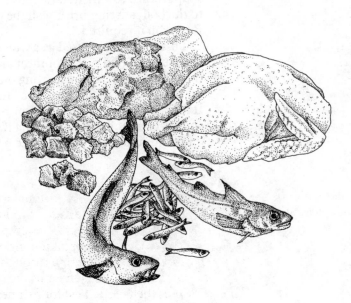

OXTAIL SOUP

Serves 4–6

700 g (1½ lb) thick end of oxtail,
  jointed
1 medium-sized onion
1 large carrot
½ turnip
1 celery stalk
25 g (1 oz) dripping
2 litres (3½ pints) basic brown stock
  (page 11)
bouquet garni
1 rasher streaky bacon, without rind
  (optional)
salt and pepper
3 tbsp plain flour
2 tbsp cream sherry (optional)

Trim any excess fat off the joints. Prepare and slice the vegetables. Heat the dripping in a heavy-based pan. Fry the joints, turning them over, for 2 minutes then add the vegetables, and fry for 4–5 minutes until the joints are browned all over. Add the stock and bouquet garni and bring slowly to the boil. Chop and add the bacon (optional). Cover the pan, lower the heat and simmer very gently for 3–4 hours until the meat is very tender. Skim off excess fat occasionally while simmering.

Strain the soup into a clean pan. Cut the meat off the bones, and mince into very small pieces. Return to the soup. Taste and season. Blend the flour with a little water and the sherry (optional), and stir in some of the soup. Stir the mixture into the main soup, return to a moderate heat, and reheat to the boil, stirring briskly all the time. Reseason if required.

This soup can be used as a winter starter without the solid pieces of meat and with a thin half-slice of lemon floating on each serving, but its main use is as a family soup. It makes a good main-course soup for supper or an informal gathering if small onion dumplings are added (see page 36).

LAMB BROTH

Serves 4–6

700 g (1½ lb) neck of lamb
1.5 litres (2½ pints) water
salt to taste
1 medium-sized carrot
1 medium-sized onion, peeled
1 small turnip
2 celery stalks
1 tbsp pearl barley
pepper
chopped parsley to garnish

For easy handling, ask the butcher to leave the lamb bone in one piece. Cut the meat off the bone, discarding any fat, and cut into small dice. Place in a large pan with the water and salt to taste, and add the bone. Bring slowly to the boil, and skim; reduce the heat and simmer for 30 minutes. Cool until the fat starts to solidify.

While cooling chop the carrot, onion and turnip, and slice the celery. Remove any fat from the broth and add the vegetables and pearl barley. Reheat to simmering point, cover, and cook very gently for 1 hour or until the vegetables and barley are soft. Reseason and stir in the parsley just before serving.

This basic broth is one of a large family. Most recipes for Scotch broth, for instance, are similar and so are some recipes for hotch potch. A good hotch potch can be made by substituting 4–6 sliced spring onions for the onion, 100 g (4 oz) young broad beans or peas (shelled) for the celery, and by adding these and half a shredded small lettuce only 30 minutes before the end of the cooking time. A bouquet garni is an improvement.

JAPANESE CHICKEN SOUP

Serves 4

100 g (4 oz) long grain rice
salt
2 raw chicken breasts
12 button mushrooms
4 spring onion bulbs
1 litre (1¾ pints) chicken stock (page 10)
¼ tsp black pepper
small pinch dry mustard
4 thin strips of lemon rind

Cook the rice in salted boiling water for 15 minutes or until just tender. Skin and bone the chicken breasts and cut the meat into thin strips about 5 cm (2 in) long. Thinly slice the mushrooms and cut the spring onion bulbs diagonally into oval rings. Bring the stock to the boil, add the chicken meat, pepper, mustard and lemon rind, cook for 5 minutes. Stir in the mushrooms and remove from the heat. Leave to stand while preparing 4 warm soup bowls. Drain the rice and divide between the bowls. Sprinkle the spring onions on the rice and place one strip of lemon rind in each bowl. Transfer the chicken and mushrooms to the bowls with a slotted spoon, then ladle in the stock.

PUREED CHICKEN SOUP

Serves 4–6

1 litre (1¾ pints) chicken stock (page 10)
125 g (4½ oz) cooked white chicken meat
2 tsp lemon juice
25 g (1 oz) butter or margarine
25 g (1 oz) flour
pinch of ground allspice
salt and pepper
chopped parsley to garnish

Skim the stock thoroughly. Cut the chicken meat into small cubes. Put about 25 g (1 oz) aside for garnishing. Purée the remainder, preferably in a food processor or blender (see page 9), with the lemon juice and enough stock to give the consistency of thin cream. Melt the fat in a pan, add the flour and cook together, stirring, for 1 minute. Slowly, stir in the remaining stock, and continue stirring until the mixture comes to the boil. Reduce the heat and simmer for 2–3 minutes. Add the chicken purée, allspice and seasoning. Reheat to simmering point, then stir in the chicken. Sprinkle with chopped parsley just before serving.

Variation
For cream of chicken soup, draw the pan off

the heat after adding the chicken. Stir a little of the hot soup into 4 tbsp single cream, then stir the cream mixture into the soup. Heat gently but do not reboil as the cream will curdle.

CHICKEN AND VEGETABLE BROTH

Serves 4

1 small boiling fowl
giblets of the bird (without liver or
*   kidneys), if available*
2 litres (3 ½ pints) water
1 onion
2 medium-sized carrots
1 celery stalk
1 tsp salt
¼ tsp pepper
2 fresh or 1 dried bay leaf
1 small courgette
2 tbsp long grain rice
4 tbsp sweetcorn, cooked and
*   drained or canned*
chopped parsley to garnish

Joint the bird and wash the giblets (if used). Place in a large pan, cover with water and bring slowly to boiling point. Peel and halve the onion, dice the carrots and slice the celery thinly. Add to the pan at boiling point with the seasoning and bay leaves. Cover tightly and simmer slowly for 3 hours. Meanwhile, dice the courgette without peeling it. Strain the broth, reserving the meat. Let the broth stand for a few minutes, then skim off the fat, and blot off any remaining droplets with soft paper. Return the broth to the rinsed pan and sprinkle in the rice. Reheat and cook gently for 15 minutes or until the rice is cooked, adding the courgette and sweetcorn 5–6 minutes before the end with some of the chicken meat, diced. Sprinkle with parsley at serving point.

The broth can be made using a chicken carcase for economy. Simmer for 1½ hours only.

FISH AND BACON CHOWDER

Serves 4

450 g (1 lb) fresh cod fillet
salt
100 g (4 oz) piece of boiling bacon
450 g (1 lb) potatoes
225 ml (8 fl oz) water
1 small onion
275 ml (½ pint) milk
150 ml (¼ pint) single cream
pepper
pinch of grated nutmeg

Skin the fish, discarding any bones. Cube the flesh and salt it lightly. Trim the rind off the bacon, and cut it into small dice. Peel the potatoes, and cut into 1 cm (½ in) cubes.

Put the water in a pan, salt lightly, and add the potatoes. Cover the pan and simmer over a low heat until the potatoes are almost tender. Draw off the heat when ready.

While cooking the potatoes, fry the diced bacon in its own fat until crisp and golden. Transfer to a plate. Chop the onion and add to the bacon fat in the frying pan. Cook until soft and beginning to brown. Scoop the onion out with a slotted spoon and add to the potatoes. Pour half the milk into the frying pan and swill it round over a low heat for a moment or two. Transfer to the pan and add the remaining milk, the cream and the fish cubes. Also add 1 tbsp of the fried bacon.

Return the chowder to a low heat, and simmer until the fish cubes are tender. Season to taste with salt, pepper and nutmeg. Serve in warmed bowls, with the remaining bacon sprinkled on top.

SHRIMP BISQUE

Serves 4–6

350 g (12 oz) cooked shelled shrimps
100 g (4 oz) softened butter
850 ml (1 ½ pints) fish stock (page 12)
2 tbsp flour
65 ml (⅛ pint) dry white wine
65 ml (⅛ pint) water
1 egg yolk
150 ml (¼ pint) single cream
salt and pepper
a few drops of lemon juice
grated nutmeg

Put 8–12 shrimps aside for garnishing. Purée the remainder in a food processor with 65 g (2½ oz) of the butter and a few spoonfuls of stock. Melt the remaining butter in a pan, add the flour and stir over a low heat for 2 minutes without colouring. Slowly stir in the remaining fish stock, wine and water; continue stirring until just boiling. Mix in the puréed shrimps, and take the pan off the heat. Beat the egg yolk into the 150 ml (¼ pint) cream and stir into the soup. Add extra cream if needed, to give the desired consistency. Season with salt and pepper, lemon juice and nutmeg to taste. Reheat if necessary, without boiling. Serve garnished with the reserved shrimps.

VEGETABLE AND PULSE SOUPS

A varied selection of appetising, nutritious and
inexpensive recipes for hot and cold soups.

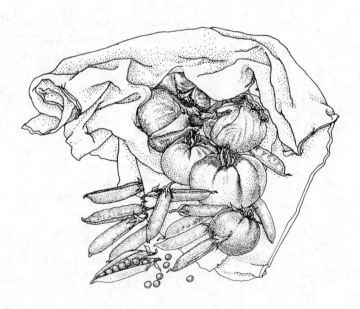

LEEK AND MUSHROOM BROTH

Serves 4

3 medium-sized washed leeks
225 g (8 oz) button mushrooms
850 ml (1½ pints) chicken stock
  (page 10)
2 tsp butter
2 tsp chopped parsley
⅛ tsp each ground black pepper,
  ground ginger and dry mustard
  powder
pinch of sugar

Strip any coarse outer sheaths from the leeks and slice both the white and tender green parts into thin rings. Remove the mushroom stems (keep them for flavouring another dish), and quarter the caps. Simmer the sliced leeks in the stock with the butter and ½ tsp chopped parsley for 6–8 minutes until soft and golden. Add the quartered mushrooms, ground spices and sugar, and cook for 4–5 minutes longer until the mushrooms soften, stirring occasionally. Serve the broth in warmed bowls, sprinkling each helping with some of the remaining parsley.

FRENCH ONION SOUP

Serves 4

225 g (8 oz) medium-sized onions
40 g (1½ oz) butter
1.5 litres (2½ pints) brown stock
  (page 11)
1 tbp plain flour
salt and pepper
4 slices bread from French stick
grated gruyère cheese

Peel and slice the onions into thin rings. Heat the butter in a pan and simmer the onions for 10 minutes until golden and beginning to brown. While frying, heat the stock to boiling point in a second pan. Stir the flour into the fat and cook gently for 2–3 minutes, stirring constantly. Take off the heat and stir in the boiling stock gradually. Return to a low heat, and simmer, uncovered for 30 minutes.

While simmering warm a tureen or 4 soup bowls (oven-proof). Place the slices of French bread in the bottom(s). Remove the bay leaf from the stock and pour the liquid into the tureen or bowls. Scatter grated cheese on each slice of floating bread. Place in the oven at 200°C (400°F) mark 6 for 7–10 minutes until the cheese has melted.

FRESH GREEN PEA SOUP WITH HERBS

Serves 4

1 small onion
1 tbsp margarine
900 g (2 lb) fresh shelled peas or
    450 g (1 lb) frozen peas
425 ml (¾ pint) chicken stock (page
    10) or classic white stock (see
    variation, page 10)
3 sprigs fresh mint, or ½ tsp dried
    mint
1 fresh basil leaf or ¼ tsp dried basil
3 sprigs fresh marjoram or 2 sprigs
    fresh thyme, or ½ tsp dried
    marjoram or ¼ tsp dried thyme
150–275 ml (¼–½ pint) milk
salt and pepper
cornflour or mashed potato (optional)
4 tbsp single cream (optional)
4 fresh mint sprigs to garnish

Peel and chop the onion, and simmer in the margarine in a pan until soft but not coloured. Add the peas and stock. Tie the fresh herbs together with thread and add to the pan, or sprinkle the dried herbs over the vegetables. Bring the stock to the boil, cover, reduce the heat and cook gently for 35–45 minutes for fresh peas, as the packet directs if using frozen peas. When the peas are soft, remove the fresh herbs and purée the soup in batches in a food processor or blender. Measure the soup and return it to the pan. Add 150 ml (¼ pint) milk and season to taste. If you wish to thicken the soup, blend 2 tbsp cornflour or potato for each 425 ml (¾ pint) soup with another 150 ml (¼ pint) milk and stir it in. Reheat the soup for about 5 minutes without boiling. Stir in the cream just before serving (optional). Garnish with fresh mint sprigs.

Variation
Green pea and shrimp soup is an attractive alternative. Fry half a stalk of chopped celery with the onion, then cook and purée the peas as above without the herbs. While cooking, simmer the shredded heart of a small lettuce and a 200 g (7 oz) can of shrimps in 150 ml (¼ pint) milk for 3 minutes, reserving a few lettuce shreds and shrimps for garnishing. Instead of thickening the soup, add the lettuce and shrimps with the flavoured milk to the puréed soup when returning it to the pan. Reheat the soup for 1 minute only, then serve with the reserved lettuce and shrimps on top.

EASY GAZPACHO

Serves 4–6

450 g (1 lb) ripe tomatoes
1 medium-sized green pepper
100 g (4 oz) onion, peeled
1 large clove garlic, peeled
1 medium-sized cucumber
2 tbsp oil
2 tbsp red wine vinegar
425 ml (¾ pint) tomato juice
salt and ground black pepper

Chop the tomatoes. De-seed and chop the pepper with the onion, garlic and cucumber. Purée the vegetables, oil, vinegar and 275 ml (½ pint) of the tomato juice in an electric blender, in batches if necessary. Turn the gazpacho into a large jug or bowl and add enough of the remaining juice to give the consistency you prefer. Season to taste. Serve in soup cups well chilled and garnished with croutons.

TOMATO SOUP

Serves 4–6

1 onion
25 g (1 oz) butter or margarine
1.2 litres (2 pints) chicken stock
  (page 10)
2 × 400 g (14 oz) cans of peeled
  plum tomatoes
2 fresh or 1 dried bay leaf
salt to taste
4 black peppercorns
strip of lemon rind
65 ml (⅛ pint) dry sherry
1 tbsp arrowroot
½–1 tsp lemon juice
4 tbsp single cream or whisked whole
  milk yoghurt
chopped parsley to garnish

Peel and finely chop the onion. Melt the fat in a pan, add the onion, and cook gently until soft but not coloured. Strain the stock, and add it with the tomatoes and their liquid, the bay leaves, salt, peppercorns and lemon rind. Mix well with a wooden spoon, squashing the tomatoes. Cover and cook gently for 45 minutes.

Pass the soup through a nylon sieve into a clean pan and add the sherry. Blend the arrowroot with 2–3 tbsp water, and stir into the soup. Reheat the soup to boiling point. Taste, add lemon juice and reseason if needed. Pour into warmed soup bowls. Swirl 1 tbsp cream or yoghurt on top of each helping just before serving and add a little chopped parsley (optional).

TOMATO SOUP WITH ORANGE

Serves 4–6

1 medium-sized onion, peeled
1 celery stalk
6 medium-sized tomatoes
   (garden-grown if possible)
1 tbsp margarine or oil
1 dried bay leaf
850 ml (1½ pints) chicken stock
   (page 10)
salt and pepper
1 tbsp cornflour
1 tbsp grated orange peel
juice of ¼–½ orange
pinch of sugar
4–6 tbsp single cream (optional)

Garnish
Finely snipped celery leaves or
   'matchstick' shreds of blanched
   orange rind

Chop the onion and celery. Quarter the tomatoes and squeeze out the seeds. Heat the margarine or oil in a pan and simmer the onion and celery for 2 minutes, stirring. Add the tomatoes, bay leaf and stock, and a light seasoning. Bring slowly to the boil, reduce the heat and simmer, half-covered, for 30 minutes. Sieve, or purée in batches in a food processor or blender. Return to the rinsed-out pan.

Cream the cornflour with a little water. Add a little hot stock, then stir the mixture into the soup. Bring to the boil, stirring all the time. Blanch the orange rind in a little boiling water for 1 minute. Stir into the soup with the orange juice, then reseason and add sugar to taste. Stir in the cream at serving point (optional), before garnishing with celery leaves or orange rind. Serve hot or cold.

CHILLED CELERY AND YOGHURT SOUP

Serves 4

3 spring onions, green and white
   parts
100 g (4 oz) small celery stalks and
   leaves
1 tbsp olive oil
425 ml (¾ pint) natural yoghurt
150 ml (¼ pint) basic vegetable
   stock (page 12)
1 tsp ground almonds or hazelnuts
pinch of sugar
salt and pepper (optional)

Chop the spring onions and celery finely in a food processor, or mince, reserving leaves. Stir in the oil over a low heat for about 5 minutes until they soften; do not let them colour. Turn into a large bowl. Cool for 2–3 minutes, then whisk in the yoghurt and remaining ingredients. Chill well before serving. Serve in chilled bowls and garnish with the celery leaves.

If the yoghurt is sharp or you prefer a thinner soup, use 275 ml (½ pint) each of yoghurt and stock.

POTAGE CRECY (CARROT SOUP)

Serves 4

450 g (1 lb) carrots
½ medium-sized onion
1 small stalk celery
¼ small turnip
1 rasher bacon without rind
15 g (½ oz) butter or margarine
1 tbsp oil
850 ml (1½ pints) brown vegetable
   stock (page 13)
bouquet garni
salt and pepper
a few drops of lemon or orange juice
3 tbsp flour
150 ml (¼ pint) milk
4 tbsp single cream or 2 tbsp cream
   and 1 egg yolk beaten together
chopped parsley to garnish

Prepare and chop all the vegetables and the bacon (a food processor is the quickest tool to use). Heat the fat and oil in a pan and fry the vegetables and bacon for 5–6 minutes, stirring constantly, until softened. Add the stock, bouquet garni, a little seasoning and the fruit juice. Cover and simmer for 30–45 minutes until the vegetables are very soft. Remove the bouquet and sieve the soup or purée in a food processor or blender, in batches. Return the purée to the pan. Cream the flour with some of the milk, add the rest of the milk, and stir into the purée. Stir over a moderate heat, until the soup boils and thickens. Taste and season. Remove from the heat, and stir in the cream or cream and egg. Return to the lowest possible heat and stir to thicken the egg yolk, but do not boil. Serve garnished with parsley.

LEEK AND POTATO SOUP

Serves 4

4 leeks, white parts only
1 medium-sized onion, peeled
25 g (1 oz) butter or margarine
2 tbsp oil
275 g (10 oz) potatoes
1 litre (1¾ pints) chicken stock (page
   10) or classic white stock (see
   variation, page 10)
salt and pepper
200 ml (7 fl oz) or 1 long life carton
   single cream

Slice the leeks and onion. Heat the fat and oil and simmer the sliced vegetables gently for 8–10 minutes, without letting them brown. While simmering, peel and slice the potatoes thinly. Add them with the stock to the simmered vegetables. Season, cover, and cook until the vegetables are soft. Sieve or purée in batches in an electric blender. Return to the pan, and reheat if serving hot; stir in the cream off the heat. If serving cold, turn into a bowl and blend in the cream and any extra seasoning you wish, then chill well, covered.

MINESTRONE

Serves 4–6

2 tbsp olive oil
2 rashers bacon without rind, cut
    into small squares, or finely diced
    cooked pickled pork
1 medium-sized onion, chopped
½ leek, finely sliced
1 clove garlic, skinned
1 celery stalk, thinly sliced
2 small potatoes, peeled and diced
    (100 g/4 oz each)
1.2 litres (2 pints) classic white stock
    (see variation, page 10)
1 large carrot, thinly sliced
50 g (2 oz) cooked or canned white
    haricot beans or fresh or frozen
    sliced green beans
3 tbsp fresh or frozen garden peas
1 tbsp chopped fresh herbs (basil,
    thyme, marjoram) or 2 tsp dried
    herbs
salt and pepper
¼ small cabbage, finely shredded
4 tbsp white or wholemeal shortcut
    elbow macaroni
3 tomatoes, skinned and cut into
    small pieces
grated Parmesan cheese

Warm the oil in a pan. Add the bacon, onion and leek, and squeeze the garlic over them. Stir over low heat for 3 minutes. Add the celery and diced potatoes, and turn in the fat, stirring constantly, for 5 minutes. Add the stock, bring to the boil and add the carrot, beans, peas, herbs and seasoning. Cover, reduce the heat and cook gently for 20 minutes. Add the cabbage, pasta and tomatoes and simmer, covered, for 20 minutes longer.

Serve a bowl of grated Parmesan cheese separately.

CREAM OF CAULIFLOWER SOUP

Serves 4

700 ml (1¼ pints) basic vegetable
    stock (page 12)
40 g (1½ oz) long grain rice
1 small onion, finely chopped or
    2 tbsp dried sliced onions
bouquet garni
pinch of grated nutmeg
1 medium-sized cauliflower
    (350 g/12 oz prepared)
150 ml (¼ pint) milk
4 tbsp whipping cream
salt and pepper

Bring the stock to the boil in a pan, add the rice, onion, bouquet garni and nutmeg, and cook for 15–20 minutes until the rice is tender. Meanwhile, cut the cauliflower head into small florets and steam over boiling water for 10 minutes or until tender; do not overcook. Reserve a few sprigs for garnishing. Add the remainder to the stock with the milk. Simmer for 5 minutes then remove from the heat. Purée the soup in batches, in a food processor or blender. If very thick, add a little more milk. Return to the pan, stir in the cream and reheat without boiling. Taste and season. Serve garnished with the reserved cauliflower sprigs.

BORSCHT (RUSSIAN VEGETABLE BROTH)

Serves 4

450 g (1 lb) raw beetroot
1 onion
1 carrot
1 turnip or ½ swede
salt and pepper
1.5 litres (2½ pints) household stock
    (see variation, page 11)
small ham bone or strip of rind from
    bacon joint
400 g (14 oz) cabbage
½ clove garlic (optional)
2 tomatoes
mashed potato (optional)
sugar
tomato purée
chopped parsley
soured cream (optional)

Peel the beetroot and cut the other root vegetables into matchsticks. Season the stock, bring to the boil with the ham bone or rind, and add the root vegetables. Cover and cook gently for 30 minutes. Meanwhile, shred the cabbage, chop the garlic (optional), and skin, de-seed and chop the tomatoes. Add the cabbage and garlic to the pan, and simmer, uncovered, for 20 minutes. Remove the ham bone or rind, add the tomatoes and cook for a further 5 minutes, adding a little mashed potato to thicken the soup slightly (optional). Flavour the soup to taste with sugar and tomato purée. Serve hot or cold sprinkled with parsley. Swirl a spoonful of soured cream on top of each serving, or serve a bowl of soured cream separately (optional).

CREAM OF BARLEY SOUP

Serves 4

275 ml (½ pint) water
50 g (2 oz) pearl barley
1.2 litres (2 pints) chicken stock
   (page 10)
1 small onion, halved
1 small carrot, quartered
25 g (1 oz) butter or margarine
1½ tbsp flour
salt and pepper
150 ml (¼ pint) single cream
65 ml (2½ fl oz) milk
1 small carrot, grated, to garnish

Bring the water to the boil, pour over the barley and leave to soak for several hours. Mix with the stock in a pan and add the onion and carrot. Cover, bring to the boil, reduce the heat and cook very gently for about 1 hour until the barley is very soft. Strain, reserving some of the barley. In a clean pan, melt the fat, add the flour and stir together for 3 minutes without colouring. Gradually stir in the stock. Bring to the boil and simmer for 5 minutes. Add the salt, pepper, cream and milk and the reserved barley. Reheat very gently, without boiling. Serve the soup in bowls with a few shreds of carrot on top of each.

As an alternative garnish place a thin ring of fine dark rye breadcrumbs around the edge of each bowl of soup, or sprinkle chopped chives on top of each bowl.

RED LENTIL SOUP

Serves 4

2 medium-sized carrots
1 medium-sized onion
1 celery stalk
2 tbsp margarine
1 tbsp oil
7 tbsp split red lentils
575 ml (1 pint) water
275 ml (½ pint) milk
good pinch of ground coriander or
   cumin
salt and black pepper
a few grains of cayenne pepper
chopped parsley to garnish

Chop the carrots, onion and celery. Simmer with the margarine and oil for 2–3 minutes, stirring constantly. Add the lentils, water, milk and seasoning. Heat to simmering point, reduce the heat, cover and cook gently for 30–45 minutes until the lentils are soft. Purée the soup in batches by sieving or in an electric blender. Return to the pan and reheat to simmering point. Taste and reseason if needed. Sprinkle with parsley just before serving.

Garnishes

Chopped fresh herbs. Rinse and dry the herb sprigs. Remove the leaves and chop finely. Squeeze in soft kitchen paper to dry and sprinkle over soup (or other dishes) just before serving. Parsley and chives are the herbs most often used.

Use mint on green pea soup, tarragon or dill on chicken and fish soups, basil or marjoram on tomato soup, and chervil on any delicately flavoured cream soup.

Chiffonade (shredded cooked green vegetables). Shred lettuce or sorrel leaves into fine ribbons. Simmer the chiffonade for a few moments in butter, drain on soft paper and add to soups just before serving. A chiffonade of sorrel is valued in French garnishing and cooking, but lettuce is more common in Britain.

Watercress, mint and other herb sprigs and leaves. Rinse and shake dry on the stem. Pick off small whole green leaves or pinch out the tiny top sprigs. Pat dry with soft kitchen paper. Scatter on any soup especially chicken or vegetable cream soups just before serving. Also beautiful on most other dishes.

Sippets. Cut day-old bread into very small 1 cm (½ in) dice. Sauté in butter, tossing well, until crisp and golden all over. Sprinkle on thick soups, or serve in a separate bowl.

Pasta and rice. Boil tiny pasta shapes or 2.5 cm (1 in) lengths of vermicelli or other thin pasta in water for 3 to 4 minutes or less. Drain, rinse in a sieve or colander and shake dry. Sprinkle on consommé or broths just before serving. (Do not cook the pasta in consommé; it will make the soup cloudy.)

Cooked long grain rice or pearl barley can be used as for pasta.

Rind strips and slices. Using a cannelle knife or a

GARNISHES A
ACCOMPANIMI

The finishing touches which will con
and enhance your soups.

sharp kitchen knife, cut thin strips lengthways, at equal intervals out of the rind of a lemon, orange or cucumber. Blanch strips of rind for a moment or two in boiling water. Cut in half and scatter on soups just before serving. (Cucumber strips are a good alternative to chopped parsley, watercress leaves or chives.) Alternatively, cut the prepared fruit into paper-thin slices and place 2 or 3 slices on each serving of soup. Lemon slices are attractive on clear soups and on fish or vegetable cream soups. Use orange slices on tomato soup.

Fried onion rings. Slice onions very thinly; dip in egg white or milk first, then in flour and sauté in a little butter until golden brown and crisp. Scatter on thick soups just before serving.

Grated hard cheese. Buy Parmesan or similar cheese in the piece if possible as the taste is quite different from that of cheese bought ready-grated. Break into small pieces before grating; big pieces will break the blades on a small cheap appliance. Sprinkle the grated cheese over soups just before serving or hand round in a separate bowl.

Soured cream or yoghurt. Whisk yoghurt until liquid. Swirl either soured cream or yoghurt on the surface of a well-coloured soup in a 'catherine wheel' ribbon. For a sophisticated flavour mix 1 tablespoon mayonnaise into 4 tablespoons soured cream before swirling on tomato soup.

Accompaniments
Serve these with soups or suitable starters.
Fairy toast. Bake very thin slices of day-old bread at 150°C (300°F) mark 2 until crisp and curled. Brown lightly under low grill heat.
Bread sticks. Cut the crusts off day-old square slices of bread. Brush the slices with melted butter, then

cut into strips. Roll some in grated Parmesan cheese, sprinkle others with onion or celery salt. Dry on a baking sheet in the oven at 180°C (350°F) mark 4 until crisp (about 15 minutes). Turn over once while drying. Serve with puréed or cream soups.

Cheese Toast Fingers. Cut square slices of day-old bread without crusts into fingers about 6 cm (2½ in) long and 2.5 cm (1 in) wide. Toast lightly on one side under the grill. Spread the untoasted sides with softened butter and a little grated cheese, and toast until golden. Serve warm.

Rolled bread and butter. Cut the crusts off a day-old tin loaf. Butter one end thinly with softened butter all over. Slice the bread very thinly. Then roll up the slice like a baby Swiss roll. Repeat the process to make more rolls. Trim the ends. Serve with cold soups or with starters such as smoked salmon or other cold fish dishes.

CHIVE OR ONION DUMPLINGS

Makes 16 dumplings

100 g (4 oz) self-raising flour
50 g (2 oz) shredded suet
1 tbsp finely chopped parsley
1 tbsp finely chopped chives or grated onion
pinch of grated nutmeg
grinding of white pepper
1 egg
2 tbsp vegetable stock (page 12)

Mix all the ingredients, except the stock, thoroughly. Add about 2 tbsp stock if needed to make a firm dough. With floured hands, roll into 16 small 'marbles'. Drop into boiling water and simmer for 4–6 minutes or until tender and swollen. Remove with a slotted spoon. Add 1 or 2 to each helping of soup. (Other finely chopped herbs can be used instead of parsley.)

STARTERS

MIXED HORS D'OEUVRE OR ANTIPASTI

A colourful and decorative selection of
easy-to-serve appetisers.

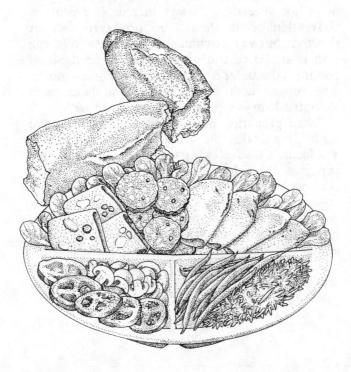

Mixed hors d'oeuvre or antipasti

Both these terms simply mean small portions of assorted cold savoury foods and preserves served 'outside', that is before, the main part of a meal. These mixed appetisers make an easy-to-serve, economical starter which can look very decorative if the items are colourful and well arranged. Kitchenware shops sell hors d'oeuvre trays holding six to nine small dishes, but it is easier to arrange a choice of five or six items on individual plates shortly ahead of the meal.

Cold cooked or salad vegetables, preserved fish such as sardines or smoked oysters, stuffed eggs, and firm savoury spreads are among the popular hors d'oeuvre foods to choose from. Select foods which differ in colour, texture and flavour from the next course; omit green beans if you serve them as your main hot vegetable. Always include one protein, conventionally it should be preserved fish or shellfish, but egg mayonnaise or a similar cold egg dish is attractive and often served instead. Sliced continental sausage or cured meat is another choice, often mixed with a vegetable. Broad beans with shredded ham is a popular Italian appetiser.

When preparing hors d'oeuvre, place one item slightly bigger than the rest in the centre of each plate as a focus; a stuffed egg (pages 63 and 64) or tomato cup (page 48) is shapely. Surround with items which contrast with this and each other in flavour and colour. Place sliced salami between green peas and golden sweetcorn for instance, not next to spicy ratatouille (page 50). Vary dressings, by using orange juice on grated carrot and a spoonful of white wine over chopped celery. Vivid garnishes, such as crumbled egg yolk on dark green spinach or chopped black olives on potato salad, add colour.

Hors d'oeuvre ingredients must look fresh and neatly trimmed, so although it is tempting, do not prepare them too far in advance. French dressing may run off salad leaves, leaving them wilted and soggy underneath. Mayonnaise may turn yellow and dull on standing. The later hors d'oeuvre are assembled, the crisper they will look.

The recipes which follow contain many items which can be used to make interesting mixed hors d'oeuvre. Use the recipes as a guide to making your own, using any home-made or bought ingredients which suit the rest of your menu.

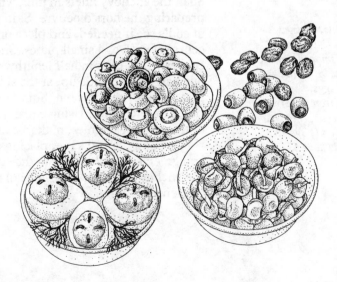

MIXED HORS D'OEUVRE FOR SUMMER

Serves 4

4 large lettuce leaves
225 g (8 oz) cooked, peeled shrimps
1 quantity eggs in jelly (page 62)
½ unpeeled cucumber, sliced
salt
175 g (6 oz) cold cooked small green
    peas
chopped mint
8 small triangles thin brown bread
    and butter
4 lemon wedges

Shred the lettuce leaves, and spread on 4 small plates. Place a small pile of shrimps in the centre of each plate. Unmould the eggs, and invert one on to each plate next to the shrimps. Arrange slices of cucumber beside the egg on one side, and sprinkle lightly with salt. Mix the peas with a little chopped mint, and place a small pile opposite the cucumber. Fill the gap between the cucumber and peas with two bread and butter triangles and a lemon wedge for squeezing.

MIXED HORS D'OEUVRE FOR WINTER

Serves 4

4 anchovy fillets, drained
milk
4 round slices smoked cod's roes
    about 1 cm (½ in) thick
2 hard-boiled eggs
tomato purée (from tube)
leeks à la Grecque, cold (page 49)
green bean salad (page 46)
Russian salad (page 47)

Soak the anchovy fillets in milk while preparing the hors d'oeuvre. Skin the slices of cod's roe if needed, and place one in the centre of each of 4 small plates. Shell the eggs, and cut each in half lengthways. Place one half egg, cut side up, at the side of each plate beside the cod's roe. Squeeze a dab of purée on each yolk. Using equal quantities of the three vegetables, make a complete ring around the cod's roe, placing the leeks and green bean salad next to the egg. Drain the anchovy fillets and curl one in the centre of each slice of roe.

FRUIT AND VEGETABLE STARTERS

A selection of well known and new recipes for
making the most of fresh fruit and vegetables.

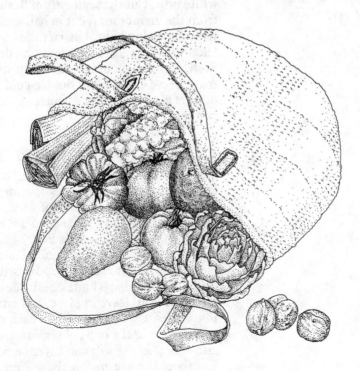

MELON AND GINGER

Serves 4

1 small honeydew melon
4 pieces preserved stem ginger in
    syrup
4 tsp syrup from the ginger jar

Cut the melon in half, scoop out and discard
the seeds. With a potato or vegetable baller,
cut the flesh into small balls. Place in
individual stemmed dessert glasses, with
any free juice. Chop the preserved ginger
very finely and scatter on the melon balls.
Pour 1 tsp of the syrup over each helping.

MELON AND ORANGE COCKTAIL

Serves 4

1 honeydew melon
2 small oranges
10 cm (4 in) piece of cucumber
2 tbsp finely chopped mint

Cut the melon flesh into small balls as for
melon and ginger (above). Place in a bowl
with any free juice. Dip the oranges into
boiling water, peel off the skins and any
white pith. Cut the segments of flesh free
from the membranes, cut in half and mix
with the melon balls. Quarter the cucumber
lengthways, remove the seeds and dice the
flesh. Mix the cucumber and mint with the
fruit. Serve chilled, but not ice-cold, in
dessert glasses. Offer a grinder of black
pepper.

Suitable types of melon to offer as a starter
are the small Charentais and Ogen melons,
large Cantaloupe and Honeydew melons, or
slices from a watermelon. Cut very small
melons in half across and scoop out the
seeds with a spoon; serve a half to each
person, cut side up, on a small plate. Cut
larger melons into segments, discarding the
seeds. With a sharp knife cut the flesh free
from the skin; leave in place, and cut across
into cubes. Offer a segment to each person,
and hand round a bowl of ground ginger
and containers of salt and cayenne pepper.
Cut slices of watermelon about 2 cm (¾ in)

thick, and cut them in half. Serve a half slice or 'fan' of watermelon to each person, with lemon segments for squeezing instead of ginger.

AVOCADO PEAR VINAIGRETTE

Serves 4

2 large firm ripe avocado pears
2 tbsp lemon juice
vinaigrette (see page 90)
watercress sprigs

Halve the pears lengthways and remove the stones. The flesh should not be discoloured or soft (see below). Brush the cut surfaces with lemon juice at once. Place a half pear, cut side up, on each of four small plates. Fill the hollows with vinaigrette sauce, and garnish the plates with watercress.

If the pears are discoloured or soft when cut open, take out the good-quality flesh in slivers, toss it with dressing and mix with cubed fresh or canned fruit (not bananas) or with salad vegetables. Serve in dessert glasses or bowls as a 'cocktail'.

AVOCADO AU FROMAGE BLEU

Serves 4

50 g (2 oz) Stilton or similar blue
   cheese with rind cut off
50 g (2 oz) low fat smooth curd
   cheese
2–4 tbsp natural yoghurt
50 g (2 oz) salted cashew nuts
2 medium-sized ripe avocado pears
lemon juice

Mash the blue cheese, then beat in the curd cheese until smooth. Add enough yoghurt to make the mixture like stiffly whipped cream. Chop the nuts into small bits and add to the mixture. Halve the pears lengthways, remove the stones and brush the cut sides all over with lemon juice. Place a half pear, cut side up, in each of four small saucers or shallow bowls. Pile the cheese and nut mixture on top.

Serve with rolled brown bread and butter (see page 36).

SHERRIED GRAPEFRUIT

Serves 4

2 large grapefruit
warmed clear honey or brown sugar
4 tsp medium-dry sherry
4 fresh pitted cherries or maraschino
    cherries

Cut the grapefruits in half across, and snip out the cores with scissors. Dig out the pips. Using a small serrated knife, cut round the fruit to separate the flesh and pith. Snip, with scissors, each side of the membrane separating the segments, but leave in place. Sprinkle the cut sides of the fruit with the honey, or sugar, and sherry. Place a cherry in the centre of each half fruit.

The grapefruit can be served hot. Sprinkle with mixed spice instead of sherry and place under the grill for about 3 minutes, or in a hot oven for 6–10 minutes. Add the fruit garnish just before serving.

PEAR CUPS WITH WALNUTS

Serves 4

2 large firm eating pears
lemon juice
50 g (2 oz) walnut pieces, chopped
100 g (4 oz) dessert dates, pitted and
    chopped
1 small round lettuce
French dressing (see page 90)

Halve the pears lengthways. Scoop out and discard the cores, then remove enough flesh to leave spoon-shaped hollows. Reserve the flesh. Brush the cut surfaces with lemon juice. Chop the reserved flesh into small pieces and mix with the walnuts and dates. Shred the lettuce finely and add a few shreds to the walnut mixture. Spread the rest of the lettuce on 4 small plates and place a pear half, hollowed side up, on each. Pare the rounded sides of the pears to make them stand level. Toss the walnut mixture with enough dressing to make it moist and glistening. Pile the mixture on the pear halves. Serve cold but not chilled.

GLOBE ARTICHOKES

Serves 4

4 globe artichokes
salt
1 tbsp lemon juice
melted butter or Hollandaise sauce
    (page 93)

Soak the artichokes upside down in cold salted water for 45 minutes to wash out any dust and insects. Lay each head in turn on the edge of a table with the stalk projecting over the edge. Bend and twist the stalk to remove it with the coarse hairs from the artichoke's base. Pare the base so that it will stand level, taking off the coarsest of the outside leaves. Square off the tips of all the remaining leaves with scissors, or slice off the top third of the whole artichoke with a sharp knife. Place the artichokes in one layer in a large pan, and pour in just enough water to cover them. Add a little salt and the lemon juice. Cover the pan and boil the artichokes for 15–45 minutes, depending on size, until a leaf pulls off easily. Turn the artichokes upside down to drain. Serve one to each person on a warmed plate. Equip each diner with paper napkins and a small spoon for removing the hairy 'choke' and eating the succulent artichoke base when the leaves have been nibbled. Supply a salad bowl for discarded leaves. Offer a warmed sauce boat of melted butter or Hollandaise sauce in which to dip the leaves.

Globe artichokes can be served with vinaigrette (page 90). They can also be stuffed. In this case, they are partly cooled after cooking. The centre cone of tender leaves is then removed to expose the choke, which must be removed. The hollowed centre is filled with a thick savoury cream dip or spread such as creamed smoked salmon.

MOULDED BEETROOT RING

Serves 4–6

1 tbsp gelatine
4 tbsp dry white wine
¼ tsp salt
225 ml (8 fl oz) boiling water
1 tsp clear honey
3 tbsp lemon juice
8–10 thin slices of cucumber
175 g (6 oz) cooked skinned beetroot
Russian salad (page 47)

Soften the gelatine in the wine in a 575 ml (1 pint) heat-proof jug. Add the salt and boiling water, and stir until the gelatine dissolves. Stir in the honey and lemon juice. Pour 4–5 tbsp of this liquid jelly into the bottom of a 700-ml (1¼-pint) ring mould. Cut the cucumber slices in half, and arrange in an overlapping ring at the bottom of the mould. Chill until the liquid jelly sets. Meanwhile, dice the beetroot. Chill the remaining jelly in the jug until it is like thick egg white. Fold in the beetroot. Spoon the mixture gently on top of the cucumber slices, making sure that all the beetroot is covered with jelly. Chill until fully set.

Dip the mould quickly in hot water to the brim. Invert a serving plate over the mould and then turn both the plate and mould over together. Jerk to free the jelly. Chill again, to firm the ring up. Fill the centre with Russian salad.

GREEN BEAN SALAD

Serves 4

350 g (12 oz) young French beans or
*   bobby beans*
1 medium-large onion
2 tbsp corn oil
1 tbsp lemon juice
salt and pepper

Top and tail the beans and string if necessary. Peel and slice the onion in very thin rings. Put the beans and onion into boiling, unsalted water and cook, covered, until the beans are just tender. Meanwhile, mix the oil, lemon juice and seasoning in a jug. Whisk well to blend. Drain the vegetables and toss in the dressing while still warm. Cool and check the seasoning before use.

This classic French starter can be served as part of a mixed hors d'oeuvre, or by itself in small dishes.

RUSSIAN SALAD

Serves 4–6

2 medium-small boiled potatoes,
  peeled and diced
200–225 g (7–8 oz) cooked
  cauliflower florets with stems
  trimmed off (from 1 small head)
4 tbsp cooked peas
3 tbsp cooked, diced carrot
2 tbsp cooked, diced turnip
50 g (2 oz) celery, diced and
  blanched (1 stalk)
1 small eating apple, peeled, cored,
  diced and dipped in lemon juice
  (optional)
1 tbsp drained capers
salt and pepper
6–8 tbsp stiff mayonnaise (see pages
  91 and 92)

Garnish
1 hard-boiled egg yolk
grated radish

All vegetables should be quite cold. To use as part of a mixed hors d'oeuvre or as a filling, season well and toss all the ingredients with enough mayonnaise to bind them. Keep in a covered bowl until needed.

To serve the salad on its own as a first course, layer some chopped egg, meat or shellfish between two layers of mixed diced vegetables in a bowl, sprinkling each layer with seasoning, and spreading thinly with mayonnaise or seasoning. Garnish with sieved hard-boiled egg yolk and grated radish.

Russian salad made just with cold cooked vegetables bound with mayonnaise is useful in a mixed hors d'oeuvre or for filling tomato cups (page 48). It tastes fresher made with home-cooked vegetables, but a mixture of canned or frozen and fresh vegetables may be more practical. To make it a complete first course, add 2 coarsely chopped hard-boiled eggs or about 100 g (4 oz) cold cooked, diced chicken meat or shellfish.

CAULIFLOWER AND WALNUT SALAD

Serves 4–6

1 small cauliflower broken into
  florets
75 g (3 oz) chopped walnut pieces
50 g (2 oz) sultanas
1 tbsp chopped fresh mint
150 ml (¼ pint) natural yoghurt
1 tbsp lemon juice
salt and pepper (optional)

Trim the ends of the cauliflower florets. Mix the florets with the walnuts, sultanas and mint in a bowl. Mix the yoghurt and lemon juice and use to bind the salad. Season to taste, adding a few more walnuts or sultanas if you wish. Serve in small chilled bowls.

MUSHROOM AND TOMATO SALAD

Serves 4

*350 g (12 oz) medium-sized button
  mushrooms
1 tbsp lemon juice or to taste
pinch of ground coriander
a few grains of curry powder
salt and black pepper
2–3 tbsp thick double cream
lettuce leaves
3–4 medium-sized firm tomatoes*

Cut the mushrooms into thin slices lengthways, trimming the stems if very long. Place the mushrooms in a bowl and toss with the lemon juice, spices and a little seasoning. Fold in 2 tbsp cream. Taste, and add extra lemon juice or seasoning if you wish, or extra cream. Place in the centre of a bed of lettuce leaves. Slice tomatoes thinly and lay in an overlapping ring around the mushrooms. Season the slices with pepper. Chill for a few moments before serving.

Alternatively, lay the lettuce leaves on four small plates. Place three or four seasoned tomato slices in the centre of each leaf and put a small pile of mushroom salad on top.

TOMATO CUPS

Serves 4

*4 firm medium-sized tomatoes
soy sauce
4 tsp thick soured cream
shredded lettuce leaves*

Filling
*4 hard-boiled eggs
3 tbsp mayonnaise
finely chopped parsley or paprika
seasoning*

Cut the tomatoes in half across. With a teaspoon, scoop out the seeds, pulp and cores. Sprinkle the hollowed tomatoes with soy sauce and turn upside down to drain. To make the filling, mash or blend the eggs with the mayonnaise, add a little finely chopped parsley and season to taste. Turn the cups right way up and fill, mounding into a dome. Top each mound with a dab of soured cream and sprinkle with parsley or paprika. Serve 2 halves to each person on small plates covered with shredded lettuce.

Filling variations
Mix 3–4 tsp finely chopped fresh herbs into 225 g (8 oz) carton of any savoury-flavoured cottage cheese.

Fill the cups with Russian salad (page 47) or spoonfuls of cold, creamy scrambled egg.

LEEKS A LA GREQUE

Serves 4–6

450 g (1 lb) young leeks

Stock
6 parsley stalks
a few coriander seeds
a few fennel seeds
1 sprig fresh or dried thyme
8 black peppercorns
1 bay leaf
2 tbsp olive oil
2 tbsp lemon juice
425 ml (¾ pint) water
¼ tsp salt
½ medium-sized onion
½ celery stalk

Prepare and wash the leeks, and cut the white stems into 5 cm (2 in) lengths (keep the green leaves for soup). Tie the herbs loosely in a muslin bag. Place all the stock ingredients in a large pan. Bring to the boil, then reduce the heat. Simmer gently for 10 minutes, add the leeks and simmer for 10–15 minutes longer. The stock should be well reduced and the leeks cooked through. Remove the onion, celery stalk and herb bundle. Turn the leeks into a warmed serving dish, if serving hot. Boil down the stock rapidly until there is just enough to coat the vegetables well. Pour over the leeks. If serving cold, leave the leeks to cool in the stock.

The style of cooking in a vegetable stock called 'à la Grecque' suits many vegetables. Any of them can be served hot or cold as part of a mixed hors d'oeuvre or as a first course on its own. Before cooking, slice courgettes, fennel hearts, celery or leeks; halve or quarter mushrooms or small onions unless tiny; quarter and de-seed cucumbers or peppers and cut in pieces; cube aubergines. Some vegetables can be served raw; they are just heated in the sauce for 2–3 minutes and served hot, or put into the hot sauce and left to cool. Vegetables which need cooking are added to the sauce for the appropriate time while it simmers.

RATATOUILLE

Serves 4–6

2 medium-sized aubergines
salt
2 large onions
1 clove garlic
1 green pepper
2–3 courgettes
4–6 tomatoes .
4 tbsp olive oil
ground black pepper
a good pinch of ground coriander
2 bay leaves
chopped parsley

Slice the aubergines thinly and cover with salt. Leave for 30 minutes. Meanwhile peel, halve and slice the onions, crush the garlic, de-seed and slice the pepper, and slice the courgettes thinly. Skin and quarter the tomatoes. Heat the oil in a large frying pan. Add the onions, garlic and pepper. Cover and cook over a low heat for 5 minutes without allowing them to brown. Drain and add the aubergine slices. Reduce the heat and simmer for 10 minutes. Add all the other ingredients. Cover again, and cook gently for 30 minutes, stirring occasionally. Remove the bay leaves. Turn the vegetables into a serving dish, if using hot.

Alternatively, cool in a covered bowl and serve cold.

ASPARAGUS

8–12 heads of asparagus per person,
   depending on thickness
melted butter or Hollandaise sauce
   (see page 93)

Scrape hard or coarse stems from the head end downwards. Trim the cut ends of the asparagus spears evenly to a length easy to cook and serve. A spear should stand upright in a jar placed inside the cooking pan with some headspace above it. Tie the spears in a bundle which will stand upright; place it, tips uppermost in a jar. Put the jar on a mat or cloth in a large pan. Pour in enough boiling water to cover all but the tips of the asparagus. Cover the pan, and cook at a medium boil for 15–20 minutes or until the spears are tender. Grasp the jar with a thick cloth and remove from the pan. Tip out the spears gently on to a cloth, untie and drain, then lay them gently on a white napkin in a warmed shallow dish. Fold the napkin over the spears until they are served.

Offer with melted butter or Hollandaise sauce served separately in a warmed jug with a spoon or small ladle.

Cook in the same way to serve cold. Cool on the cloth, then use as required.

Asparagus as a starter by itself is best served hot but is useful as a cold garnish or as a part of a mixed hors d'oeuvre .

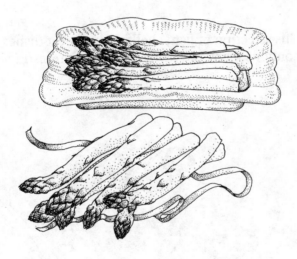

FISH, SHELLFISH AND MEAT STARTERS

This selection of fish, shellfish and meat dishes contains many old favourites with interesting variations.

SMOKED TROUT OR MACKEREL

Serves 4

4 whole fish or fillets
lemon wedges
watercress sprigs
horseradish sauce
shredded lettuce (for fillets)

If you have whole fish, skin them. It is usual to leave the head and tail on, but these can be removed if you wish. Lay the fish on plates and garnish with the lemon wedges and watercress. Offer horseradish sauce and bread and butter separately.

Skin fillets with care; if thin, they may break up. Lay them, flesh side up, on shredded lettuce, then garnish and treat like whole fish.

SMOKED SALMON

Serves 4

8 slices of smoked salmon
lemon wedges
watercress to garnish

If possible, buy freshly sliced smoked salmon. For serving as it is, the salmon should be cut in paper-thin slices from the tail and towards the head. Serve the slices flat or folded, with lemon wedges, a grinder of black pepper, and thin brown bread and butter. Garnish with watercress.

Thicker scraps of smoked salmon from coarser parts of the side can be shredded and used to make pâtés, mousses, omelettes, etc. Smoked salmon and scrambled egg is another classic 'hot and cold' starter (see page 54).

SMOKED SALMON AND SCRAMBLED EGGS

Serves 4

4 large thin slices of smoked salmon
6–8 eggs, depending on size of
  salmon slices
butter
milk
salt and pepper

Spread the smoked salmon slices flat on a tray. Scramble the eggs, with the butter, milk and seasoning, by your usual method; they should still be quite moist. Spread the scrambled egg over the salmon slices, then roll up the slices like Swiss rolls. Lay on a warmed platter and serve at once with a bowl of soured cream and a plate of rolled bread and butter (see page 36).

Variation
For small pieces or trimmings of smoked salmon, make the dish as follows:
Use 175–225 g (6–8 oz) salmon, 8 eggs and 150 ml (¼ pint) fresh double cream instead of soured cream. Reserve a few small neat pieces of salmon for garnishing and shred the remainder. Make the scrambled eggs with 1 tbsp of the cream, adding the shredded salmon; the consistency should be soft and creamy. Heat the remaining cream to simmering point. Garnish the eggs with the reserved salmon, and cover with hot cream. Serve immediately.

SALMON COCKTAIL

Serves 4

175 g (6 oz) cooked, fresh or canned
  salmon without skin or bone
1 tbsp dry white vermouth
150 g (5 oz) unpeeled cucumber
100 g (4 oz) full fat soft cheese
1 tsp lemon juice
salt and pepper

Drain the salmon if necessary, and flake roughly. Sprinkle with vermouth and divide between 4 dessert glasses. Cut 4 thin slices of cucumber for garnishing and set aside. Cut the remaining cucumber into chunks. Place the chunks with the cheese and lemon juice into a food processor or blender and process until the cheese is a pale green cream with tiny pieces of cucumber. Season to taste.

Spoon the cucumber cream over the salmon. Chill. Just before serving, cut the reserved cucumber slices into butterflies or other decorative shapes, and place one on each cocktail.

OYSTERS ON THE HALF SHELL

Buy oysters from a reliable fish supplier and make sure they are tightly closed. If possible, ask an expert to open them just before serving. If you prepare them at home, scrub them well, then open as follows. Hold each in turn in a cloth or gloved hand, with the deeper shell downwards; work the point of a sharp knife into the hinge between the shells, then cut the ligament which holds them together. (You can buy a special oyster knife for doing this.) Open the oyster carefully, remove its beard, and loosen it from the shell but leave it in place. As a rule, serve 6 oysters in the deep shells to each person. Arrange them on plates, season lightly, and supply lemon wedges, Tabasco sauce or cayenne pepper, a grinder of black pepper and thin brown bread and butter. Small oysters, fresh or canned, can be used in cooked 'au gratin' and similar dishes, or can be mixed with a little cream sauce as a filling for vol-au-vents, patties etc.

Canned smoked oysters are removed from the can, piled on small plates, then served with lemon wedges, black pepper and thin brown bread and butter.

Smoked sprats are arranged on plates and served in the same way.

TARAMASALATA

Serves 4

175 g (6 oz) smoked cod's roe,
   skinned
2 small cloves garlic, peeled
25 g (1 oz) soft white breadcrumbs
3 tbsp lemon juice
4–5 tsp olive oil
2 tsp cold water
black pepper

Place the cod's roe in a bowl and squeeze
the garlic over it. Mash with the
breadcrumbs and lemon juice until free of
lumps. Gradually whisk in the olive oil and
water alternately to the consistency and
flavour you prefer, and season. The mixture
should be creamy but not too liquid or it
will separate on standing. Chill well. Serve
in small bowls with warmed pitta bread and
lemon wedges.

Taramasalata can also be used as a spread or
dip, depending on the consistency.

SALADE NICOISE

Serves 4–6

lettuce leaves
225 g (8 oz) cooked, cooled new
   potatoes
2 medium-sized tomatoes, skinned
   and sliced
1 tsp chopped fresh basil
1 tsp chopped parsley
grated rind of 1 lemon
100 g (4 oz) cooked, cooled French
   beans
50 g (2 oz) black olives
2 hard-boiled eggs, quartered
8 anchovy fillets, drained and split
   lengthways
French dressing (page 90) with a
   squeeze of garlic

Make a bed of lettuce leaves on a flat platter.
Slice the potatoes and arrange on the lettuce
with the tomato slices. Sprinkle with the
herbs and lemon rind. Pile the French
beans in the centre of the dish or scatter
over it. Halve and stone the olives and chop
into fairly large bits, sprinkle over the salad.
Add the quartered eggs. Arrange the
anchovy fillets in a lattice pattern on top.
Sprinkle the salad well with the dressing,
and leave to stand for 30 minutes before
serving, to let the flavours blend. Serve with
brown bread and butter.
   This is an attractive salad dish with its
contrasting colours if well arranged.

MARINATED HADDOCK

Serves 4

2 tbsp dried, sliced onions
350 g (12 oz) raw smoked haddock
    fillet, skinned
1 tsp chopped fresh mixed herbs as
    available (not mint)
black pepper
juice and grated rind of 1 large
    lemon
3 tbsp olive oil
lettuce leaves

Soak the onions in scalding water for
5 minutes. Cut the haddock fillet into short
thin strips and lay side by side in one or two
flat (non-metal) dishes. Drain the onions
and scatter them on top. Sprinkle with
herbs and pepper. Mix the lemon juice, rind
and oil in a jug and pour over the haddock.
Cover and marinate for 12–24 hours in a
cool place, turning the strips over
occasionally. Lay the fillet strips on lettuce
leaves spread on small plates, and serve with
wholemeal bread and butter.

SEAFOOD TOWERS

Serves 4

2 small hard-boiled eggs
2 × 215 g (7½ oz) can red salmon
5 tbsp mayonnaise (see pages 91 and
    92)
1 tsp tomato ketchup
1 large firm tomato
2 flat soft rolls
butter for spreading
salt and black pepper
paprika

Shell the eggs, cut them in half across, and
set aside. Drain the salmon and mash it with
the mayonnaise and ketchup until well
blended. Cut the tomato across into four
slices, discarding the ends. Split the rolls
and butter. Pile a quarter of the salmon
mixture on the buttered side of each roll,
and flatten it into a thick layer. Place a
tomato slice on top, and season it well. Cap
with half an egg, cut side down; sprinkle a
little paprika on top. Serve one 'tower' on
each of four small plates.

POTTED SHRIMPS

Serves 4–6

225 g (8 oz) unsalted butter
400 g (14 oz) peeled shrimps
4 tsp ground cloves
¼ tsp ground mace
¼ tsp white pepper
melted clarified butter

Melt the butter in a pan. Add all the other ingredients except the clarified butter. Heat gently, stirring, until well blended. Turn into small ramekins and cool. When cold cover with melted clarified butter and chill until firm. Serve one to each person with lemon wedges and brown bread and butter.

CHICKEN AND SHRIMP COCKTAILS

Serves 4

2 tsp dried sliced onions
4–6 lettuce leaves
150–175 g (5–6 oz) cooked white
  chicken meat without bone
50 g (2 oz) cooked or canned peeled
  shrimps
2 tsp finely chopped parsley
1 tsp lemon juice
¼ tsp Worcestershire sauce
3 tbsp double cream
150 ml (¼ pint) mayonnaise (see
  pages 91 and 92)
salt and pepper

Soak the dried sliced onions in boiling water for 5 minutes. Tear up the lettuce leaves and use to line 4 dessert bowls or stemmed dessert glasses. Dice or chop the chicken meat. Drain and add the onion. Set 12–16 shrimps aside for garnishing, and add the remainder to the chicken with the parsley. Stir the lemon juice, Worcestershire sauce and cream into the mayonnaise, and season to taste. Mix with the chicken and shrimps. Divide between the bowls or glasses, and garnish with the reserved shrimps.

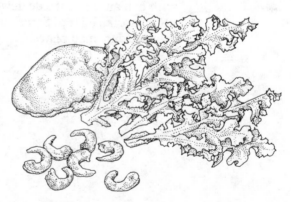

CHAUDFROID OF CHICKEN

Serves 4

*4 small cooked chicken breasts
  skinned and boned (about 65 g
  (2½ oz) when prepared)
4 tbsp aspic jelly (page 16)
4 tbsp thick mayonnaise, chilled (see
  pages 91 and 92)
4 pimento-stuffed olives
lettuce leaves*

Trim the chicken breasts neatly, and place on a wire cooling rack over a baking sheet. Place the aspic jelly in a heat-proof jug. Stand the jug in hot water and stir until the jelly dissolves. Remove from the heat. Place the mayonnaise in a chilled bowl, and stir in the melted jelly little by little until evenly blended. Chill until the mixture reaches a thick coating consistency. Slice the olives into three rounds each, discarding the ends.

Spoon the thick mayonnaise mixture over the chicken pieces. Leave in a cool place until almost set, then garnish each piece with three olive slices. Leave to set firmly. Arrange the chicken pieces on lettuce leaves laid on individual plates.

The chaudfroid sauce is equally good on white fish fillets or cold, poached salmon cutlets or pieces. Garnish with capers.

SNAILS

Serves 4

*coarse salt
215 g (7½ oz) can snails
24–30 Burgundy snail shells
1 quantity garlic butter (see page 93)*

Heat the oven to 200°C (400°F) mark 6. For each person, cover a large deep plate with a thick layer of coarse salt, and make hollows for 6–8 snail shells. In the same way, prepare with salt a large baking sheet which will hold all the snail shells. Drain the snails and put one (or two if tiny) in each shell. Tuck them well in. Cover thickly with the garlic butter. Place the shells, open side up, in the hollows on the baking tray. Place in the oven for 6 minutes or until the butter is melted and very hot. Using frying tongs or a cloth, transfer the snails to the plates and serve at once with hot dry toast.

MELON WITH PARMA HAM

Serves 4

1 firm, ripe honeydew melon (or other green-fleshed melon)
12 slices Parma or Westphalian ham

Cut 16, 6 × 2 cm (2½ × ¾ in) sticks of melon. Arrange four sticks diagonally on each individual serving plate. Loosely roll-up 12 slices of ham. Place a roll of ham between each melon stick.
Serve with brown bread and butter.

HAM AND ALMOND ROLLS

Serves 4

1 large firm eating pear
juice of ½ lemon
100 g (4 oz) full fat soft (cream) cheese
25 g (1 oz) browned flaked almonds (see page 93)
salt and pepper
4 large thin slices cooked ham

Garnish
2 firm tomatoes, quartered
small lettuce leaves

Peel, halve and core the pear. Cut into 1 cm (½ in) cubes. Toss in lemon juice, coating completely, and drain. Set aside.
Sieve the cheese into a bowl. Fold in the pear cubes and browned almonds. Season. Lay the ham slices flat, and place a quarter of the filling across the one end of each slice. Roll up the slices around the filling. Trim the ends of the rolls neatly. Lay on small plates garnished with tomato quarters and lettuce leaves.
Serve with thin brown bread and butter.

CHOPPED LIVER

Serves 4–6

450 g (1 lb) chicken livers
salt
175 g (6 oz) onions, peeled
2 tbsp chicken fat or oil
3–4 hard-boiled eggs
salt and pepper

Garnish
lettuce leaves
sliced tomatoes

Rinse the chicken livers, cut into small pieces and salt well. Grill until they give off no more blood. Chop the onion, and fry in the chicken fat or oil until soft but not brown. Finely mince together the livers, onion and two or three hard-boiled eggs. Season well and mix to a paste with a little of the frying fat if needed. Shape into a mound or block. Chop the remaining egg finely and sprinkle on the liver in an attractive pattern. Garnish the base of the mound with lettuce and tomato.

EGG AND CHEESE STARTERS

A variety of easy-to-prepare dishes which need
little or no cooking.

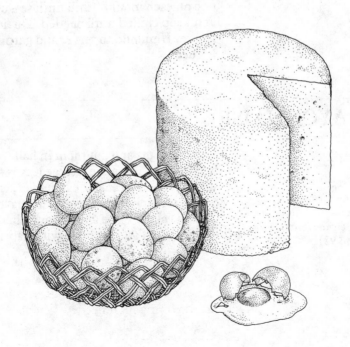

EGGS IN JELLY

Serves 4

firmly jellied consommé (page 14)
4 round slices pimento-stuffed olive
2 hard-boiled eggs, shelled
4 round slices of firm liver sausage,
   slightly larger than the moulds
   used
lettuce leaves

Measure how much consommé is needed by filling 4 round, flat-bottomed moulds three-quarters full with water. The moulds should be deep enough to hold half an egg with about 1 cm (½ in) headspace. Warm the consommé just enough to melt it. Cool until quite cold but not yet setting. Pour a thin layer into each mould, and place a slice of olive in the centre. Chill until set. Cut the eggs in half across, and place one in each mould, cut side down. Fill the moulds with enough consommé to come about half-way up the sides. Chill again until set. Then fill the moulds almost to the top, covering the eggs. Chill until almost set. Trim the slices of liver sausage to fit the moulds, and lay one on each mould. Chill until set, cover, and keep chilled until needed. Do not freeze. Unmould to serve, and garnish with lettuce.

EGG MAYONNAISE

Serves 4

4 hard-boiled eggs
4 large flat lettuce leaves
8 anchovy fillets
150 ml (¼ pint) mayonnaise (see
   pages 91 and 92)
paprika

Shell the eggs and cut them in half lengthways. Place the lettuce leaves on 4 small plates. Arrange 2 egg halves, cut side down, on each plate. Spoon the mayonnaise over the eggs. Place an anchovy fillet on each egg half and sprinkle with paprika.

EGGS WITH CHEESE-TOMATO

Serves 4

4 tbsp mayonnaise (see pages 91 and
   92)
4 tbsp full-fat soft (cream) cheese or
   Philadelphia
½ tsp tomato purée (from tube)
¼ tsp dried tarragon
2 tsp tomato juice
1–2 drops lemon juice (optional)
lettuce leaves
4 hard-boiled eggs
chopped parsley to garnish

Beat together until smooth the mayonnaise, soft cheese, tomato purée, tarragon, tomato juice and lemon juice (optional). Shred a few lettuce leaves and spread them as a bed on 4 small plates. Cut the eggs in half across, and place 2 halves, cut side down, in the centre of each plate. Spoon the cheese-tomato mayonnaise on top and garnish with chopped parsley.

Chopped fresh tarragon and mayonnaise made with tarragon vinegar give an extra fresh flavour.

ANCHOVY-STUFFED EGGS

Serves 4

8 anchovy fillets, drained
milk
8 capers
6 hard-boiled eggs
1 tbsp softened butter
½ medium-sized cucumber, thinly
   sliced or thin rounds of buttered
   brown bread
salt
2 wide lemon wedges cut in half
   across, to garnish

Soak the anchovy fillets in a little milk for 15 minutes. Drain. Chop the fillets finely with the capers. Shell the eggs, cut in half lengthways and remove the yolks. Mash the yolks to a paste with the anchovies, capers and butter. Cut a sliver off the rounded bottom of each white so that it stands level. Fill the hollowed whites with the anchovy-yolk mixture. Arrange the cucumber or bread slices in a bed on 4 plates, sprinkle lightly with salt and arrange 3 egg halves, cut side up, on each bed in a tricorne shape. Place a piece of lemon, skin side up, in the centre of each tricorne.

HERB-STUFFED EGGS

Serves 4

6 hard-boiled eggs
6 medium-sized tomatoes, thinly
    sliced
a few drops of vinegar
black pepper
chopped parsley

Filling
1 tsp lemon juice
2 tbsp mayonnaise (see pages 91 and
    92)
2 tbsp softened butter
1 tbsp finely snipped chives
1 tbsp finely chopped fresh herbs
    (thyme, marjoram, parsley or
    savory)
½ tsp dry mustard powder
½ tsp salt
a few grains of chilli powder

Shell the eggs and cut them in half across.
Scoop out the yolks. Mash the yolks with all
the filling ingredients. Cut a sliver off the
rounded bottom of each white so that it
stands level. Pile in the filling, mounding it
high.

Arrange the tomato slices in a bed on each
of 4 small plates. Sprinkle with the vinegar,
pepper and parsley. Arrange 3 egg halves,
cut side up, on each bed and sprinkle with a
little more pepper if you wish.

If possible, use fresh, new-laid eggs for
boiling hard. The raw whites are thick and
viscous, and fill most of the shell. With age
or in warm conditions, the whites become
thin and watery, the air space at the
rounded end enlarges, and the yolk no
longer rests in the centre of the egg.

PRINCESS COCKTAILS

Serves 4

1 quantity curry mayonnaise (see
    page 92)
2 tbsp seedless raisins
150 g (5 oz) gruyère cheese in one
    piece
2 rings pineapple canned in natural
    juice
1 tbsp flaked almonds
4 maraschino cherries, drained

Make the lightly curried mayonnaise (see
page 92).

Pour boiling water on the raisins and
leave to stand for 5 minutes. Cut the cheese
into 1 cm (½ in) dice. Drain the pineapple
and cut each ring into 12 segments.

Divide the mayonnaise between 4
stemmed dessert glasses. Drain the raisins
and mix all the salad ingredients except the
cherries. Pile on top of the mayonnaise and
top each 'cocktail' with a cherry.

MOCK CRAB

Serves 4

3 hard-boiled egg yolks
2 tbsp corn oil
1 tsp onion salt
1 tsp clear honey
1 tsp mixed English mustard
1 tbsp white wine vinegar
225 g (8 oz) Red Leicester cheese,
    shredded on the coarsest holes of a
    grater
2 tbsp cooked white chicken meat,
    minced or shredded
lettuce leaves
tomato purée (from tube)

Sieve the egg yolks. Keep 1 rounded tbsp yolk aside for garnishing. Work the rest to a smooth paste with the oil, using the back of a spoon. Mix in the onion salt, honey and mustard. Blend thoroughly. Gradually add the vinegar to make a smooth, semi-liquid sauce.

Mix the cheese and chicken lightly with a fork, keeping the cheese shreds separate. Mix in the sauce lightly. Chill well.

Lay the lettuce leaves in a bed on a shallow oval dish. Spread the mixture in a slightly mounded layer on top. Garnish with thin lines of sieved egg yolk and tomato purée piped from the tube. Serve on to small plates at the table and offer hot dry toast.

TOMATOES WITH BLUE BRIE CREAM

Serves 4

1 leek, white stem only
salt
8 firm medium-sized tomatoes
2 small celery stalks from centre of
    head
pepper
100 g (4 oz) blue Brie-style cheese
    with rind scraped off
2 tbsp double cream
¼ tsp grated spring onion
4 tbsp French dressing (page 90)

Slice the leek finely and blanch in lightly salted boiling water for 4 minutes until tender. Drain and cool. Cut off the smooth ends of the tomatoes and carefully take out the seeds and cores with a teaspoon. Drain upside down.

Dice the celery finely and season lightly. Work the cheese with the back of a spoon until soft, then work in the cream. Chop and add 2 tbsp of the leek. Mix with the celery.

Fill the hollowed tomatoes with the cheese-celery mixture. Replace the tops if you wish. Scatter the remaining leek on 4 small plates, and place the tomatoes on top, cut side up. Mix the grated onion into the French dressing, and spoon it over them.

TOMATO ASPIC MOULDS

Serves 4

2 tbsp gelatine
725 ml (1¼ pints) tomato juice
a few drops of Worcestershire sauce
  or lemon juice (optional)
salt and pepper
75 g (3 oz) Mozzarella cheese

Garnish
1 bunch washed watercress

Soften the gelatine in 150 ml (¼ pint) cold tomato juice. Heat the remaining 575 ml (1 pint) juice in a pan. Take off the heat, and stir in the softened gelatine. Stir until the gelatine has dissolved. Flavour with Worcestershire sauce (optional) and season to taste. Pour about a third of the aspic into a 725-ml (1¼-pint) ring mould, or 4 individual moulds. Chill until set. Keep the remaining mixture at room temperature.

Cut the cheese into 1 cm (½ in) dice. When the chilled juice is firm, scatter with the cheese cubes. Cover with the remaining juice which should be cooled but still liquid. Chill again until firm. Unmould on to a serving plate or small plates, and garnish the centre of a ring mould with the watercress. Use a few sprigs to scatter round individual moulds.

Liver sausage rolled into marble-sized balls or diced cooked vegetables can be used instead of cheese.

PATES AND MOUSSES

An interesting selection of pâtés and mousses,
ranging from housekeeper's pâté to anchovy
mousse.

It is seldom practical to make a pâté for just 4–5 people. Both pâtés and mousses are rich dishes, and the quantity needed for 4 first-course helpings would be too small to garnish and display attractively as a single dish. It is more usual therefore to make a larger quantity which will serve at least 6–8 people and to expect to serve it at a second meal. Most pâtés freeze perfectly if required.

INSTANT SALMON PATE

Serves 4

450 g (1 lb) cold cooked salmon
    without skin or bone or one 440 g
    (15½ oz) can of red salmon
5 tbsp softened unsalted butter
1 tbsp sherry
½ tsp bottled anchovy sauce
pinch of ground mace
salt and pepper
4 thick slices of cucumber

Drain the canned salmon and remove any bone. Flake fresh or canned salmon. Pound, or beat with an electric mixer to reduce to shreds (a food processor tends to reduce it to a grainy purée). Beat in 1–2 tbsp of the butter, then the sherry, anchovy sauce and mace; season very lightly. Beat in the remaining butter, then taste and adjust the seasoning. Turn into 4 individual pots or ramekins, level the tops and chill to firm up. Meanwhile, salt the cucumber slices well and place on a tilted plate for 30 minutes. Pat dry with soft paper. Chop the slices finely, and pat dry again. Sprinkle on the pâté just before serving.

SMOKED MACKEREL PATE

Makes 600 g (1¼ lb) pâté

50 g (2 oz) unsalted butter in small
  knobs
450 g (1 lb) smoked mackerel fillets
salt and black pepper
1 tbsp tomato purée
2 tbsp double cream
2 tbsp lemon juice
2 tbsp finely chopped fresh parsley
pinch of ground mace
a few grains of cayenne pepper

Soften the butter. Skin the fish fillets, discarding any bones. Mash the fish, and season lightly. Put the fish with half the butter, and the tomato purée in a liquidiser or food processor. Blend until just mixed. Slowly, add the remaining butter and the other ingredients in order, blending briefly after each addition. Purée to the consistency you prefer, then taste and reseason if needed. Turn into a suitable container, taking care to knock out any air-holes. Cover and chill, use within 36 hours, or freeze for up to 1 month.

CHICKEN AND MUSHROOM PATE

Serves 4–6

450 g (1 lb) chicken meat (white or
  brown) without skin or bone
100 g (4 oz) lean pork
2 streaky bacon rashers without rind
100 g (4 oz) pork sausage meat
40 g (1½ oz) soft white breadcrumbs
175 g (6 oz) button mushroom caps,
  chopped
1 small onion, chopped
1 tomato, de-seeded and chopped
2 tsp finely chopped fresh herbs (not
  mint) or 1 tsp dried mixed herbs
1 egg
salt and black pepper

Grease an 18 × 9 × 6 cm (7 × 3½ × 2½ in) loaf tin, and heat the oven to 170°C (325°F) mark 3. Mince together the chicken meat, pork and bacon rashers. Mix together the minced meat and sausage meat in a bowl. Work in the breadcrumbs, mushrooms, onion and tomato. Add the herbs. Beat the egg until liquid and use to bind the pâté mixture. Season to taste and turn into the tin, pressing well down into the corners. Cover tightly with greased foil.

Stand the loaf tin in a baking tin, and pour in cold water to a depth of about 1 cm (½ in). Place in the oven and bake for 1–1½ hours until the pâté begins to shrink and any free fat is translucent. Pour off the free fat, and leave the pâté in a cool place under a light weight for several hours until quite cold. Chill until needed. Turn out and serve in slices or squares with hot toast and butter.

HOUSEKEEPER'S PATE

Serves 4–6

175 g (6 oz) cooked game meat
  without skin and bone
175 g (6 oz) cooked brown chicken
  or turkey meat
100 g (4 oz) thick gammon or bacon
  rashers without rind
4 tbsp game or strong chicken stock
2 tbsp brandy
4 tbsp softened butter
salt and black pepper
a few grains of cayenne pepper
75 g (3 oz) small mushrooms,
  coarsely chopped
2 spring onions greens

Cut the game and poultry meat into small
pieces, discarding any bone splinters and
gristle. Cut the gammon or bacon into small
pieces. Fry the gammon pieces in their own
fat, until cooked through and lightly
browned. Remove, leaving the fat in the
pan. Place all the meat in a food processor
or blender and process until finely
shredded, in batches if necessary. Add the
stock and brandy while processing. Stop the
machine, add the butter and process again
until well blended. Season to taste.

If you do not have a processor or blender,
mince the meats 2 or 3 times, then work in
the liquids and butter to make a well
blended mixture, and season.

Put the chopped mushrooms and
1 chopped spring onion top in the frying
pan, and simmer in the bacon fat until soft.
Grease with butter a 18 × 9 × 6 cm
(7 × 3½ × 2½ in) loaf tin. Turn in half
the meat mixture and press down evenly
making sure that the corners are filled.
Scatter the mushrooms and spring onion on
top. Cover with the remaining meat mixture
in an even layer. Cover and chill until
wanted. Turn out to serve, and garnish with
the remaining finely chopped spring onion
green. Serve this low-fat pâté with brown
bread and butter or offer apricot chutney.

LIVER PATE

Makes 900 g (2 lb)

lard for greasing
350 g (12 oz) belly of pork without
   rind
450 g (1 lb) pig's liver or pig's liver
   and chicken livers, mixed
3 shallots, finely chopped
50 g (2 oz) soft white breadcrumbs
2 tbsp chopped parsley
½ tsp ground ginger
good pinch of grated nutmeg
2 tsp salt
¼ tsp ground black pepper
1 tbsp brandy
1 tbsp port or Madeira
2 tbsp double cream
3 fresh bay leaves

Choose an oblong terrine, deep baking dish or loaf tin which has a capacity of 1.2 litres (2 pints). Grease well with lard. Place in a baking or roasting tin, and pour enough water into the tin to reach half-way up the sides of the dish. Remove the dish, and place the tin on the centre shelf of the oven. Heat the oven to 180°C (350°F) mark 4.

Cut the meat and liver into small pieces, removing any gristle, tubes or membrane. Mince the meats together three times, using the finest cutter, or process in batches in an electric blender until smooth. Mix in thoroughly all the other ingredients except the bay leaves. Press the pâté firmly into the dish, leaving no air pockets. Level the top, and arrange the bay leaves diagonally in the centre. Cover the dish tightly with greased foil and place in the tin in the oven, and bake for 1½–1¾ hours. When done, the pâté will have shrunk slightly and its fat and juices will run clear yellow when the top is pressed. Cool the pâté under an even weight, then chill for 24–48 hours before cutting. Serve from the dish, garnished with chopped parsley, or turn out and place on a serving dish. Cut in slices for serving.

Variation
Pack a good half of the pâté evenly in the dish, then add a 3 mm (⅛ in) layer of seasoned cooked spinach, well drained and pressed dry, before the rest of the pâté.

COLD EGG MOUSSE

Serves 6–8

4 tbsp aspic jelly (see page 16)
5 hard-boiled eggs
salt and pepper
pinch of paprika
a few drops of Worcestershire or
    Harvey's sauce
2 tsp sherry
175 ml (6 fl oz) double or whipping
    cream
chopped parsley

Garnish
chopped aspic jelly

Melt the jelly in a heat-proof jug standing in hot water. Chill until cold but still liquid. Meanwhile, separate the eggs. Reserve the whites, and sieve the yolks into a bowl. Mix in a sprinkling of salt and pepper, a pinch of paprika and the Worcestershire or Harvey's sauce and sherry. Stir or beat in the liquid aspic to make a smooth liquid mixture; chill until gummy. Meanwhile, chop the egg whites into very small pieces and whip the cream until semi-stiff and about 275 ml (½ pint) in volume.

Fold the whipped cream into the egg-yolk mixture so that no streaks remain; beat it briefly if necessary. Fold in the chopped whites. Turn the mixture into a 700 ml (1¼ pint) soufflé dish, and chill until set. Garnish with chopped aspic jelly. Serve from the dish, with hot dry toast.

TWO-CHEESE MOUSSE

Serves 4–6

2½ tsp gelatine
3 tbsp cold water
150 g (5 oz) Brie
4 tbsp double cream
5 tbsp milk
100 g (4 oz) cottage cheese, sieved
2 egg whites
4 thin slices of cucumber to garnish

Soften the gelatine in the water in a heat-proof container. Stand the container in scalding hot water and stir until the gelatine dissolves. Set aside.

Cut the rind off the cheese as thinly as possible. Cut the cheese paste into small pieces if solid. Beat with an electric or hand mixer, gradually adding the cream, milk and cottage cheese, or put them all into a food processor, and process briefly until smooth. Beat in the gelatine mixture or add it to the processor and blend in. If made in a processor, turn into a bowl.

Whisk the egg whites until they are fairly stiff. Stir 1–2 tbsp into the cheese mixture to loosen it, then fold in the rest as lightly as possible. Turn the mixture gently into a soufflé dish and chill until set. Shortly before serving, cut the cucumber slices in half and use to garnish the top of the mousse. Serve from the dish with rolled brown bread and butter (page 36).

ANCHOVY MOUSSE

Serves 4

50 g (2 oz) can anchovy fillets, drained
milk
3 hard-boiled egg yolks
6 tbsp mayonnaise (see pages 91 and 92)
3 tbsp double cream
a good pinch of chilli powder
2 raw egg whites
chopped parsley to garnish

Cover the anchovy fillets in milk and soak for 15 minutes; drain, and chop finely. Place all the ingredients except the egg whites in a food processor or blender, and blend until almost smooth. There will still be tiny flecks of anchovy in the 'cream'. Turn the mixture into a bowl. Whisk the egg whites stiffly and stir 1 tbsp into the anchovy mixture. Fold in the remainder. Turn the mixture very gently into 4 decorative small bowls and chill for at least 2 hours. Garnish with a little chopped parsley and serve with fingers of hot dry toast.

PASTRY, PANCAKES AND PASTA STARTERS

Versatile pastry, pancake and pasta recipes
which are popular and easy to make.

Pasta and pancakes are both popular and convenient as a first course. Modern 'instant' pasta takes only 4 minutes to cook, and with a simple sauce or just melted butter and grated cheese is one of the easiest hot starters to offer. Pancakes can be made ahead, frozen, and thawed in moments. After filling, they can be reheated in a low oven without any attention. Half the usual quantity of pasta or 1 pancake per person is usually enough as a starter course.

FILLED PUFFS

Makes 24–30 puffs

150 ml (¼ pint) water
50 g (2 oz) butter
8 tbsp self-raising flour
2 whole eggs and 1 white, beaten

Heat the oven to 220°C (425°F) mark 7. Place the water and butter in a pan, and bring to the boil. Have the flour ready in a bowl, and tip it all in. Beat vigorously over the heat until the paste forms a ball which leaves the sides of the pan cleanly. Beat in the eggs and egg white little by little, incorporating as much air as possible; an electric mixer is helpful. Beat until the mixture is glossy. Place 2 cm (¾ in) dessert spoons of the mixture on a non-stick baking sheet, spacing well apart. Bake for 15 minutes or until the puffs are well risen and golden brown; do not underbake. Slit the side of each puff, and remove any damp filling with a teaspoon. Return damp puffs to the oven for 2–3 minutes. Cool the puffs, then freeze or store in an airtight tin.

Fill with any mild creamy cheese or anchovy mousse (page 73).

RICH SHORTCRUST PASTRY

225 g (8 oz) plain flour
pinch of salt
150 g (5 oz) butter
2 egg yolks
a little cold water if needed

Heat the oven to 200°C (400°F) mark 6.
Sieve the flour and salt into a bowl and rub
in the butter. Beat the egg yolks. Make a
well in the flour, add the egg yolks and mix
well. Gradually draw down the flour from
the sides and work it all in with the tips of
the fingers. It should be a firm yet soft
dough, so add a teaspoon or two of cold
water if necessary. Cover and leave to cool
and relax.

Line the flan ring or tart case with pastry
rolled to a thickness of about 5 mm (¼ in).
Poke down into the ring or tart case using a
little ball of pastry as a pusher. Line with
greaseproof paper and fill with baking beans
or any other beans. Bake blind for 15
minutes, remove the beans and paper. Bake
for a further 10 minutes to dry out.

CREAM AND PRAWN FLAN

Serves 6–8

18–20 cm (7–8 in) pastry flan case,
    baked blind (see rich shortcrust
    pastry above)
175 g (6 oz) cooked, peeled prawns
    or 215 g (7½ oz) can of prawns
    in brine
salt (optional)
150 g (5 oz) full fat soft (cream)
    cheese
65 ml (2½ fl oz) white wine
4 tsp gelatine
120 ml (4 fl oz) whipping cream
chopped parsley

Lightly salt the prawns, or drain the can
and pat dry. Spread evenly over the bottom
of the flan case. Then make the topping.
Cream the cheese with the back of a spoon
in a bowl. Pour the wine into a heat-proof
jug adding the gelatine to soften. Stand the
jug in hot water and stir until the gelatine
dissolves. Remove the jug from the heat.
Allow to cool slightly while half-whipping
the cream. Beat or stir the gelatine mixture
into the cheese thoroughly, then fold in the
cream. Quickly, spread the cream-wine
mixture evenly over the prawn filling. Chill
until needed, then sprinkle with chopped
parsley. Serve this rich flan in small wedges.

Filling Variations
(1) For salmon filling, spread 175 g (6 oz) of 'instant' salmon pâté (page 68) over the base of the flan case.
(2) To make a mushroom filling slice 225 g (8 oz) button mushrooms thinly. Sauté in a little butter and oil until lightly browned, then drain on soft paper. Spread over the base of the flan case.

Individual vol-au-vents are always popular as a hot starter. The cases can be home-made or bought. Ready-baked ones are sold in packets. Frozen ones may be uncooked, ready for baking, or fully baked; uncooked cases are sometimes hazardous to use as they are designed to rise high, and may topple over in the oven if not baked with care.

Any smooth filling which can be heated briefly is suitable for vols-au-vent. For instance, the cheese filling for pancakes on page 80 could be used, or the same sauce made with 75 g (3 oz) minced cooked white chicken meat or finely chopped prawns instead of cheese. Season prawns with allspice instead of nutmeg.

LEEK TART

Serves 4–6

18–20 cm (7–8 in) pastry tart case,
  baked blind (see rich shortcrust
  pastry, page 76)
225 g (8 oz) sliced white leek stems
  (from 3 medium-sized leeks)
3 tbsp butter or margarine
2 large or 3 small eggs
150 ml (¼ pint) single cream or milk
pinch of grated nutmeg
salt and pepper
25 g (1 oz) grated gruyère cheese

Heat the oven to 190°C (375°F) mark 5. Cook the sliced leeks in the minimum of boiling water for 5–7 minutes until soft. Drain, return to the dry pan and toss in 2 tbsp of the fat until well coated. Take off the heat. Beat the eggs, cream or milk, and seasonings together in a bowl. Stir in the leeks with any fat. Turn the mixture gently into the pastry case, spreading the leeks evenly. Sprinkle with the cheese. Dot with the remaining fat. Bake for 20–25 minutes until the custard is lightly set in the centre. Serve hot.

PANCAKES

Makes 12–14 pancakes

4 tbsp butter or margarine
225 g (8 oz) plain flour
175 ml (6 fl oz) water
175 ml (6 fl oz) milk
4 eggs
½ tsp salt

Melt the fat and set to one side. Sift the flour, then re-measure.

If possible make the batter an hour before it is needed. For speed and smoothness, use a blender if possible.

To make the batter using a blender, put the liquids, eggs, salt, flour and melted fat into the goblet in order, then cover and blend at top speed until quite smooth. Stop the machine, push down any bits of flour or batter sticking to the walls of the goblet, and blend again briefly. Leave to stand in a cool place.

To make the batter with a hand beater, beat the eggs into the sifted flour, then beat in the liquid gradually, followed by the melted fat and salt. Strain the batter to remove any lumps and leave in a cool place for an hour or more.

Spices, herbs or other flavourings, or even well-chopped solid ingredients can be added to a pancake batter if you wish.

Just before use, test the consistency of the batter. If it is thicker than pouring cream, blend or beat in 1–2 tbsp water.

To make the pancakes, brush a shallow 15 cm (6 in) frying pan or pancake pan with oil. Heat it to very hot, then reduce the heat. Lift the pan off the heat. Pour in and swirl round just enough batter to cover the whole pan thinly. (If you are quick, you can pour any excess batter back into the container.) Replace the pan on the heat and shake gently for about 1 minute. Loosen the pancake with a round-ended palette knife, and flip it over; the underside should be patched with brown. Brown the second side for about 15 seconds, then lift the pancake off the pan and transfer to a sheet of greaseproof paper. Oil the pan again and repeat the procedure to make more pancakes.

You will probably not be able to make all the pancakes one after another because any heavy pancake pan gets too hot. If the batter sets before running all over the pan's surface, cool the pan for a moment or two and thin the batter slightly with water.

Stack the pancakes as you make them in piles of 6 or 8, putting thick and thin pancakes in separate piles. Thicker pancakes are more suitable for savoury fillings, thin pancakes for sweet ones. Wrap securely and freeze. They thaw in moments in a low oven.

SAVOURY PANCAKE GATEAU

Serves 6

*six 15 cm (6 in) pancakes, a little
thicker than sweet pancakes (see
page 78)*

Fillings
1 *4 hard-boiled eggs, chopped,
bound with 5–6 tsp soured
cream or thick yoghurt
salt and pepper*
2 *3 large firm tomatoes, thinly
sliced, sprinkled with chopped
fresh or dried basil
salt and pepper*
3 *5 tbsp low-fat soft curd cheese
mixed with ¼ finely chopped
green pepper
salt and pepper*

Topping
*65 ml (⅛ pint) soured cream or
whisked whole milk yoghurt
chopped parsley*

Heat the oven to 170°C (325°F) mark 3. Mix
the three fillings in separate bowls. Lay one
pancake flat on a heat-proof serving plate.
Cover evenly with half filling 1. Lay a
second pancake on top, and cover it with
half filling 2. Add a third pancake and
spread with all filling 3. Repeat the layers,
using fillings 2 and 1. Top with the last
pancake. Cover with greased foil, and
reheat for about 15 minutes. Warm the
soured cream or yoghurt slightly, and spoon
on top of the pancake stack. Sprinkle with
parsley.

To serve, cut in wedges at the table.

PANCAKES WITH CHEESE FILLING

Serves 4

*four 15 cm (6 in) pancakes, a little
thicker than sweet pancakes (see
page 78)
1 tbsp grated gruyère cheese*

Filling
*ground black pepper
pinch of grated nutmeg
75 g (3 oz) grated gruyère cheese
1 egg
150 ml (¼ pint) milk
1½ tbsp flour*

Prepare an oblong heat-proof serving platter
which will hold the folded pancakes side by
side. Reheat the pancakes in a low oven if
made ahead and keep them warm under
greased foil. Mix a grinding of pepper and
the nutmeg into the cheese; set aside.
Whisk together the egg, milk and flour in a
pan. Place over low heat and whisk until the
mixture comes to the boil; cook for 2–3
minutes until the sauce is thick. Take off
the heat and whisk in the seasoned cheese.

Lay the pancakes flat. Place a good 2 tbsp
sauce in a strip along the centre of each
pancake. Fold both sides of the pancake

over it. Lay the pancakes side by side on the platter. If any sauce remains, spoon it over, then sprinkle with the cheese. Place under the grill for a moment or two, to soften the cheese topping. Serve at once.

NOODLES WITH MUSHROOM SAUCE

Serves 4

225 g (8 oz) egg noodles (tagliatelle)
1 tbsp butter or margarine

Sauce
1 small onion, peeled
2 tsp butter or margarine
2 tsp oil
1 tsp chopped parsley
1 tsp flour
175 g (6 oz) button mushrooms,
*   thinly sliced*
8 tbsp chicken stock (page 10) or as
*   needed (use a stock cube if you*
*   have no home-made stock)*

Boil the pasta according to the packet directions. Drain, and keep warm. For the sauce, chop the onion finely. Heat the fat and oil in a pan, and fry the onion and parsley until the onion softens, stirring constantly. Sprinkle in the flour. Stir in the mushrooms and 6 tbsp of the stock. Simmer, stirring until the mushrooms soften. This should make enough liquid for a few spoonfuls of slightly thickened sauce. If not add a little more stock. Turn the pasta into a warmed dish, and toss with 1 tbsp fat. Spoon the sauce over it.

ASSORTED HOT STARTERS

A combination of fish, vegetable and egg dishes
which make good hot starters and need very
little attention.

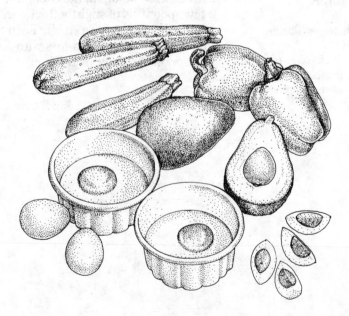

A baked fish or vegetable dish makes a good hot starter, needing no attention while it cooks. Hot egg dishes are light and luscious, provided the main course is an easy one; the eggs can be cooked in a few minutes as a rule, but it must be done at the last moment. (The Middle Eastern egg 'bake' on page 84 is an exception.)

EGGS IN CREAM

Serves 4

4 eggs (new-laid if possible)
2 hard-boiled eggs
150 ml (¼ pint) double cream
pinch of paprika
salt and black pepper

Warm 4 individual ramekins or small bowls. Hard-boil the new-laid eggs for the minimum time; crack and place under running water immediately. Hold each egg in turn in a cloth, shell and quarter them.

While the eggs cook, shell those that are already hard-boiled. Discard the whites (or keep them for a soup garnish). Crumble the yolks.

Pour the cream into a small pan, and add the paprika and seasoning. Bring to the boil very slowly and simmer, stirring, until the cream thickens (within 2 minutes). Tip in the quartered eggs and turn in the cream to coat. Spoon 4 egg quarters into each ramekin or bowl with some cream sauce. Garnish with crumbled egg yolk.

EGGS VAUDOISE

Serves 4–6

2 tbsp butter
50 g (2 oz) cooked, peeled shrimps
6 eggs
salt and pepper
3 tbsp dry white French vermouth
browned almonds (page 93)

Melt the butter and allow to cool slightly. Drain the shrimps. Beat or whisk the eggs in a bowl with seasoning to taste. While beating, trickle in the melted butter, then the vermouth. Turn the eggs into a frying pan, and scramble them over very low heat until almost set. Remove from the heat and stir in the shrimps. Turn into a warmed shallow dish, and sprinkle with a few browned almonds. Serve into small shallow dishes at the table and offer hot dry toast.

MIDDLE EASTERN EGG BAKE

Serves 4–6

175 g (6 oz) courgettes
salt
1 medium-sized onion
½ de-seeded sweet red pepper
2 tbsp butter or margarine
1 tbsp oil
4 eggs
1 tbsp chopped parsley
black pepper

Heat the oven to 170°C (325°F) mark 3. Cut the courgettes into 3 mm (⅛ in) slices. Sprinkle with salt and place on a tilted plate for 15 minutes. Drain and pat dry. Chop the onion and pepper finely. Heat 1 tbsp fat and the oil in a frying pan which will hold all the vegetables, and stir-fry the onion and pepper until soft. Add the remaining fat and sliced courgettes and stir until they are soft and golden. Drain the vegetables on soft paper.

Butter generously the inside of an 18-cm (7-in) oven-proof pie plate or dish, about 4 cm (1½ in) deep suitable for serving. Beat the eggs in a bowl and add the vegetables and parsley; season to taste. Turn the mixture into the dish. Cover tightly with a lid or foil, and bake for 30 minutes. Uncover and bake for another 10 minutes or until the dish is firm in the centre. Serve from the dish in squares, slices or wedges.

In the Middle East, beaten eggs are often mixed with meat or vegetables and baked or fried slowly, using low heat, until firmly set. The savoury egg 'cake' may be served in small wedges, squares or slices as a convenient first course.

PLAICE ROLLS WITH SHRIMPS

Serves 4

4 fresh plaice fillets
200 g (7 oz) cooked peeled shrimps
25 g (1 oz) soft white breadcrumbs
a pinch of ground mace
25 g (1 oz) softened butter
salt and pepper
3 tbsp dry white wine
120 ml (4 fl oz) fish stock (page 12)
*   or water*
4–5 tbsp double cream
rolled bread and butter (page 36)
lemon wedges

Heat the oven to 180°C (350°F) mark 4. Skin the plaice fillets. Reserve 16–20 shrimps for garnishing and chop the remainder. Mix with the breadcrumbs, mace and softened butter to make a stuffing. Season lightly. Spread the stuffing on the skinned sides of the fillets and roll up from the tail end. Place, cut side down, in a shallow, greased baking dish. Pour the wine and fish stock or water over the fish. Cover loosely and bake for about 20 minutes. Meanwhile heat the cream. Place the stuffed rolls on 4 small warmed plates, spoon a little hot cream over each and garnish with the reserved shrimps. Serve hot, with rolled bread and butter and lemon wedges.

If you prefer use the liquid in which the fillets are cooked to make a white sauce to pour over instead of using cream.

BAKED WHITING IN FOIL

Serves 4

4 small whiting
salt and pepper
50 g (2 oz) butter or margarine
lemon juice

Garnish
chopped parsley
lemon wedges

Heat the oven to 180°–190°C (350°–375°F) mark 4–5. Clean the fish if required, cut off the head and fins, and trim the tails square. Rinse inside and out, and pat dry with soft paper. Lay each fish on a rectangle of foil large enough to enclose it. Season the fish inside, dot with fat, and sprinkle with lemon juice. Make a 'parcel' of each fish by folding the edges of the foil together over it, and twisting the foil at the head and tail ends. Lay the foil 'parcels' on a baking sheet. Bake for 20–25 minutes. To see if ready, run a poultry skewer through the foil into the fish which should be tender to the touch of the skewer. To serve, remove from the foil to warmed plates, pour any juices in the package over the fish and sprinkle with chopped parsley. Offer lemon wedges for squeezing.

Whole small fish such as trout, red mullet or whiting baked in foil make a good hot first course because they are simple to prepare and serve, and need no attention while cooking. If the oven is needed for the main course, they can be baked in odd free corners or kept warm for a while on the oven floor without cross-flavouring other foods or creating cooking odours. They can either be presented as 'parcels' at the table, or be transferred to warmed plates for serving.

WHITE FISH SOUFFLE

Serves 4–6

225 g (8 oz) cooked whiting or other
    delicate white fish
1 tbsp grated onion
2 tbsp butter or margarine
50 g (2 oz) grated cheese
2 tbsp cornflour
275 ml (½ pint) milk
2 eggs, separated
1 egg white
salt and pepper

Heat the oven to 200°C (400°F) mark 6. Oil the inside of a 1.2-litre (2-pint) soufflé or similar dish. Flake the fish in a large bowl. Simmer the grated onion with 2 tsp of the fat until soft, and mix with the fish. Mix in the cheese.

Put the cornflour in a heat-proof jug, and blend with a little of the milk. Heat the remainder of the milk to boiling point with the remaining fat. Stir into the cornflour mixture. Return the mixture to the pan and heat, stirring constantly, until it boils and thickens. Remove from the heat, and stir into the fish mixture. Stir in the egg yolks and season well. Whisk all the egg whites stiffly and fold into the mixture. Turn into the dish, and bake for 25 minutes until well risen and coloured. Serve immediately.

CRUMBED AVOCADOS

Serves 4

2 firm avocado pears
lemon juice or French dressing (see
    page 90)
100 g (4 oz) cooked smoked cod or
    haddock
a few drops of oil
3–4 tbsp soft breadcrumbs
2–3 tbsp butter, melted
lemon wedges

Heat the oven to 180°C (350°F) mark 4. Cut the avocados in half lengthways and remove the stones. If the stones are small or the surrounding flesh discoloured, scoop out a little of the flesh. Immediately brush the cut sides of the pears with lemon juice or French dressing. Flake the fish, removing any skin or bones, and mix with a few drops of oil, using just enough to hold the shreds of fish together. Pile the fish into the avocado halves, covering them. Sprinkle the whole surface with breadcrumbs and the melted butter. Place in a baking tin and bake for 20 minutes until well heated through. Serve at once with lemon wedges.

BAKED COURGETTES

Serves 4

6 *small courgettes, about 10 cm*
  (4 in) long
salt
6 finely chopped shallots
2 tbsp soft fine breadcrumbs
pepper
2 tbsp butter
6 lean back bacon rashers
watercress sprigs

Heat the oven to 180°C (350°F) mark 4. Slice the courgettes in half lengthways, and simmer in lightly salted water for 5 minutes. Drain and place cut side up on a baking sheet. Cover the cut surfaces with the chopped shallots and sprinkle with the breadcrumbs and salt and pepper. Dot with the butter. Lay the bacon rashers flat, removing any rind and fat, and cut 2 long, lengthways strips of lean meat off each rasher; they should cover the courgettes, and overhang the ends. Lay one strip on each courgette half. Place in the oven and bake for about 25 minutes until the bacon is brown and crisp. Serve 3 courgette halves to each person, arrange in a pattern on small plates with a garnish of watercress sprigs.

DRESSINGS AND ACCOMPANIMENTS

This chapter shows how to make a variety of
basic sauces and dressings with some
accompaniments.

FRENCH DRESSING

Makes 50 ml (2 fl oz)

2–3 tbsp corn or groundnut oil
pinch of dry mustard powder
salt and pepper
1 tbsp white wine vinegar or 2 tsp
   vinegar and 1 tsp lemon juice

Mix the oil with the seasonings in a bowl. Stir or beat in the vinegar and juice (optional), drop by drop until an emulsion forms. Stir or beat again just before use.

Alternatively, shake the oil and seasonings in a screw-topped jar, add the vinegar and juice and shake again vigorously. Repeat just before use.

Many cooks believe that olive oil and malt vinegar are too heavy and strongly flavoured for dressing fruits or delicate green salad leaves. They are best kept for dressing strongly flavoured vegetables and leaves such as chicory or endive. A dressing for fruits is best made partly with lemon juice.

VINAIGRETTE

Makes 100 ml (3 fl oz)

2–3 tbsp corn or groundnut oil
pinch of dry mustard powder
salt and black pepper
1 tbsp white wine vinegar
½ tsp finely chopped chives
½ tsp finely chopped parsley
½ tsp finely chopped fresh dill,
   tarragon or chervil
1 tsp finely chopped capers
1 tsp finely chopped pitted green
   olives or gherkin

Mix the oil and seasonings and stir or beat in the vinegar drop by drop as for French dressing (above). Add the flavourings, mix well, and leave to stand for 1–2 hours before use.

MAYONNAISE (WHISK OR MIXER)

Makes 350 ml (12 fl oz)

275 ml (½ pint) corn or soya oil
3 egg yolks
1 tbsp white wine vinegar or lemon juice
½ tsp salt
¼ tsp dry mustard powder

Make sure all the ingredients are at room temperature. Warm the oil slightly until just tepid. Set to one side.

Rinse a mixing bowl in hot water, and dry thoroughly. Put in the egg yolks and beat for 2 minutes or until the yolks thicken. Add the vinegar, salt and mustard, and beat for another half minute. Still beating constantly and steadily, add the oil drop by drop until the liquid in the bowl thickens. From time to time beat without adding extra oil to make sure that all the oil is being absorbed. When the mixture thickens, add the oil a little more quickly, but continue beating constantly until the mayonnaise is the desired consistency, or all the oil has been added.

To prevent the mayonnaise curdling, beat in 1 tbsp boiling water at the end. Beat in extra seasoning to taste, if you wish.

To cure thinned or curdled (separated) mayonnaise
Rinse a clean bowl in hot water and dry. Add 1 tbsp of the mayonnaise and 1 tsp *made* mustard. Beat together until the mayonnaise thickens. Beat in 1 tsp more mayonnaise. When it is incorporated and thick, repeat the process, adding the mayonnaise in small spoonfuls, until it has all been added and has thickened.

Pour the completed mayonnaise into a bowl, cover tightly, and store until required in the refrigerator.

Olive oil can be used but it is heavy and slightly more difficult to mix in smoothly than a lighter oil. A flavoured oil such as garlic oil, or a herb-flavoured vinegar makes a pleasant change.

MAYONNAISE (BLENDER)

Makes 425 ml (¾ pint)

1 egg
½ tsp salt
¼ tsp dry mustard powder
*1 tbsp white wine vinegar or lemon
   juice*
*225 ml (8 fl oz) corn or soya oil, or as
   needed*

Break the egg into the blender goblet, add the seasonings, and blend at top speed until foaming and thickening. Blend in the vinegar or juice. With the motor running, add the oil through the hole in the lid drop by drop until the mayonnaise thickens, then slightly faster. The mayonnaise will stiffen quickly, and will be thicker than if made with a whisk.

Beat in 1 tbsp boiling water at the end, to prevent from curdling, and any extra seasoning to taste.

A flavoured oil or vinegar can be used in place of the corn or soya oil.

CURRY MAYONNAISE

1 tsp lemon peel
2 tbsp lemon juice
1 tsp clear honey
½ tsp curry paste
*6 tbsp mayonnaise (see page 91 and
   above)*

Grate the lemon; squeeze and strain the juice. Mix the peel and juice with the honey and curry paste in a small bowl. Stir in the mayonnaise by spoonfuls, blending thoroughly.

HOLLANDAISE SAUCE

2 tbsp white wine vinegar
1 tbsp water
2 egg yolks
75 g (3 oz) butter or as needed, cut
  into small bits
salt and pepper

Place the vinegar and water in a small pan, bring to the boil and reduce to about 1 tbsp. Cool slightly then pour into a heat-proof basin over a pan of very hot water. Whisk in the egg yolks and one at a time, continue whisking until the mixture thickens. Whisk in the butter, one bit at a time, blending thoroughly. Season to taste. If the sauce is too sharp, whisk in another 25 g (1 oz) of butter. The sauce, when ready, should just hold its shape. Serve while still warm (but not hot).

GARLIC BUTTER

2 cloves garlic, peeled
2 tbsp finely chopped spring onion
  bulb
3 tbsp white wine
2 tbsp finely chopped parsley
150 g (5 oz) unsalted butter, cut into
  knobs
1 tbsp lemon juice (or to taste)
salt and black pepper

Squeeze the garlic over the onion in a small pan. Add the wine. Simmer over a very low heat until the wine has evaporated. Remove the pan from the heat, mix in the parsley, then beat the mixture into the butter. Continue beating while adding a little lemon juice and seasoning. Taste and adjust the flavour if needed. Press into a pot, cover, and refrigerate until needed.

BROWNED ALMONDS

1 tsp butter
1 tsp oil
25 g (1 oz) flaked almonds

Heat the butter and the oil in a small pan over a gentle heat. Add the flaked almonds and stir constantly until they start to brown. Take the pan off the heat at once, stir until the almonds are light gold. Transfer at once to soft paper and toss to drain, then cool.

WHAT IS THE WI?

If you have enjoyed this book, the chances are that you would enjoy belonging to the largest women's organisation in the country — the Women's Institute.

We are friendly, go-ahead, like-minded women, who derive enormous satisfaction from all the movement has to offer. This list is long — you can make new friends, have fun and companionship, visit new places, develop new skills, take part in community services, fight local campaigns, become a WI market producer, and play an active role in an organisation which has a national voice.

The WI is the only women's organisation in the country which owns an adult education establishment. At Denman College, you can take a course in anything from car maintenance to paper sculpture, from book-binding to yoga, or cordon bleu cookery to fly-fishing.

All you need to do to join is write to us here at the **National Federation of Women's Institutes, 39 Eccleston Street, London SW1W 9NT**, or telephone 01-730 7212, and we will put you in touch with WIs in your immediate locality. We hope to hear from you.

ABOUT THE AUTHOR

Maggie Black has been writing about cookery for many years. Her career in this field began when she joined Ward Lock Ltd to edit *Mrs Beeton's Cookery and Household Management*. Since then she has written about smoking foods, barbecuing and, in particular, the folklore of food and traditional dishes. Recently, she has been working on cooking for health, especially for elderly people, concentrating on vegetable cookery and lighter meals.

INDEX